What is the '101' **series**?

At Alan Rogers, we know that readers have many and diverse interests, hobbies and particular requirements. And we know that our guides, featuring a total of some 3,000 campsites, can provide a bewildering choice from which it can be difficult to produce a shortlist of possible holiday destinations.

The Alan Rogers 101 guides are devised as a means of presenting a realistic, digestible number of great campsites, featured because of their suitability to a given theme.

This book remains first and foremost an authoritative guide to excellent campsites which are ideal for holidays with younger children, typically under the age of 12.

101 **Best campsites for children**

Campsite life is made for children. They love the freedom, the space, the ability to run around and explore. And of course there's ample opportunity for getting grubby - and the chances of a bath are slim which is even better news for most under 12s.

For parents there's the deeply comforting notion that seeing your little treasures sleeping deeply at the end of a day in the fresh air is a far better option than seeing them slumped over a techno-gadget in a stuffy bedroom, whether at home or in a soulless hotel.

And of course we all fancy the idea of a child enjoying the 'fun and ice creams' side of the holiday while also learning a little about the big wild world and the forces of nature, meeting flora and fauna close up and personal, interacting with others and perhaps taking on a little social responsibility.

G000114901

101 best campsites

for **children**

2012 EDITION

Compiled by: Alan Rogers Guides Ltd

Designed by: Vine Design Ltd

© Alan Rogers Guides Ltd 2011

Published by: Alan Rogers Guides Ltd,
Spelmonden Old Oast, Goudhurst, Kent TN17 1HE

www.alanrogers.com
Tel: 01580 214000

British Library Cataloguing-in-Publication Data:
A catalogue record for this book is available from
the British Library.

ISBN 978-1-906215-66-8

Printed in Great Britain by
Stephens & George Print Group

Welcome to the Alan Rogers
'101' guides

The Alan Rogers guides have been helping campers and caravanners make informed decisions about their holiday destinations since 1968. Today, whether online or in print, Alan Rogers still provides an independent, impartial view, with detailed reports, on each campsite.

With so much unfiltered, unqualified information freely available, the Alan Rogers perspective is invaluable to make sure you make the right choice for your holiday.

contents

Alan Rogers – in search of 'the best'

Alan Rogers himself started off with the very specific aim of providing people with the necessary information to allow them to make an informed decision about their holiday destination. Today we still do that with a range of guides that now covers Europe's best campsites in 27 countries.

We work with campsites all day, every day. We visit campsites for inspection purposes (or even just for pleasure!). We know campsites 'inside out'.

We know which campsites would suit active families; which are great for get-away-from-it-all couples; we know which campsites are planning super new pool complexes; which campsites offer a fantastic menu in their on-site restaurant; which campsites allow you to launch a small boat from their slipway; which campsites have a decent playing area for kicking a ball around; which campsites have flat, grassy pitches and which have solid hard standings.

We also know which are good for fishing, golf, spas, children, nature and outdoor activities; which are close to the beach; and which welcome dogs. These particular themes form our '101' series.

All Alan Rogers guides (and our website) are respected for their independent, impartial and honest assessment. The reviews are prose-based, without overuse of indecipherable icons and symbols. Our simple aim is to help guide you to a campsite that matches best your requirements – often quite difficult in today's age of information overload.

What is the **best**?

The criteria we use when inspecting and selecting sites are numerous, but the most important by far is the question of good quality. People want different things from their choice of campsite, so campsite 'styles' vary dramatically: from small peaceful campsites in the heart of the countryside, to 'all singing, all dancing' sites in popular seaside resorts.

The size of the site, whether it's part of a chain or privately owned, makes no difference in terms of it being required to meet our exacting standards in respect of its quality and it being 'fit for purpose'. In other words, irrespective of the size of the site, or the number of facilities it offers, we consider and evaluate the welcome, the pitches, the sanitary facilities, the cleanliness, the general maintenance and even the location.

Expert opinions

We rely on our dedicated team of Site Assessors, all of whom are experienced campers, caravanners or motorcaravanners, to visit and recommend campsites. Each year they travel around Europe inspecting new campsites for Alan Rogers and re-inspecting the existing ones.

When planning
your **holiday...**

A holiday should always be a relaxing affair, and a campsite-based holiday particularly so. Our aim is for you to find the ideal campsite for your holiday, one that suits your requirements. All Alan Rogers guides provide a wealth of information, including some details supplied by campsite owners themselves, and the following points may help ensure that you plan a successful holiday.

Find out more

An Alan Rogers reference number (**eg FR12345**) is given for each campsite and can be useful for finding more information and pictures online at www.alanrogers.com

Simply enter this number in the 'Campsite Search' field on the Home page.

Campsite descriptions

We aim to convey an idea of its general appearance, 'feel' and features, with details of pitch numbers, electricity, hardstandings etc.

Facilities

We list specific information on the site's facilities and amenities and, where available, the dates when these facilities are open (if not for the whole season). Much of this information is as supplied to us and may be subject to change. Should any particular activity or aspect of the campsite be important to you, it is always worth discussing with the campsite before you travel.

Swimming pools

Opening dates, any charges and levels of supervision are provided where we have been notified. In some countries (notably France) there is a regulation whereby Bermuda-style shorts may not be worn in swimming pools (for health and hygiene reasons). It is worth ensuring that you do take 'proper' swimming trunks with you.

Charges

Those given are the latest provided to us, usually 2011 prices, and should be viewed as a guide only.

Toilet blocks

We assume that toilet blocks will be equipped with a reasonable number of British style WCs, washbasins and hot showers in cubicles. We also assume that there will be an identified chemical toilet disposal point, and that the campsite will provide water and waste water drainage points and bin areas. If not the case, we comment. We do mention certain features that some readers find important: washbasins in cubicles, facilities for babies, facilities for those with disabilities and motorcaravan service points.

Reservations

Necessary for high season (roughly mid-July to mid-August) in popular holiday areas (i.e. beach resorts). You can reserve many sites via our own Alan Rogers Travel Service or through other tour operators. Remember, many sites are closed all winter and you may struggle to get an answer.

Telephone numbers

All numbers assume that you are phoning from within the country in question. From the UK or Ireland, dial 00, then the country's prefix (e.g. France is 33), then the campsite number given, but dropping the first '0'.

Opening dates

Dates given are those provided to us and can alter before the start of the season. If you intend to visit shortly after a published opening date, or shortly before the closing date, it is wise to check that it will actually be open at the time required. Similarly some sites operate a restricted service during the low season, only opening some of their facilities (e.g. swimming pools) during the main season; where we know about this, and have the relevant dates, we indicate it – again if you are at all doubtful it is wise to check.

Accommodation

Over recent years, more and more campsites have added high quality mobile homes, chalets, lodges, gites and more. Where applicable we indicate what is available and you'll find details online.

Special Offers

Some campsites have taken the opportunity to highlight a special offer. This is arranged by them and for clarification please contact the campsite direct.

Calling
all **kids**

There are thousands of campsites across Europe. Many are fine for children but some really are exceptional. It's not just a question of plonking down a playground or having a couple of small bikes for hire. There should be a willingness to give children that little bit more, a positive rather than a passive attitude towards welcoming youngsters, and the ability to see children as bringing life and soul to the campsite, rather than being a potential nuisance or cause of damage. This guide features a short-list of just 101 campsites that go out of their way to welcome children and give them the time of their lives.

What's in it **for the kids**

Whatever their age, children love camping. They enjoy the fun and novelty of it all; they can make dens, play hide and seek games – and all in a safe environment. There are plenty of other children to play with (having to amuse the kids is not usually a problem when camping!). And of course, being a holiday, there's a good chance of going to bed later than usual.

Much of campsite life is geared towards children, making life more relaxing for all. It's a cliché, but if the kids are happy then mum and dad are too.

Taking **it easy**

It's all about families doing what they want, when they want. Take a midday wander around a campsite and you'll find children splashing in the pool, toddlers enjoying the swings before lunch. Some excited jabbering in the distance might herald the arrival of the Kids' Club trooping by on their treasure hunt. Over in the corner, under a shady tree, mum and dad sit in companionable silence, quietly getting stuck into their paperbacks.

For some it's barbecue time; for others it's not long since they were breakfasting in pyjamas. Some, young and old, are getting ready for an afternoon nap, while others are planning a trip to the beach, a pony ride, an ice cream treat… There are choices for everyone and it really doesn't matter, there's no fixed itinerary – this is camping.

Animal **magic**

We all know kids love animals. And campsites, with plenty of space and often rural locations, are ideal for being home to farmyard animals such as goats, chickens, ducks, ponies and donkeys. It is not unknown for the most popular feature on some sites to be the small animal enclosure, not the state of the art pool complex with all its waterslides and water-based excitement.

for the **active**

Children want action and there's nowhere better to find it than on a campsite. Many campsites offer a range of activities, ranging from simple home-spun pursuits (think fossil hunting on a Dorset beach or an on-site treasure trail) to impressive sports facilities and supervised activities (perhaps junior quad biking or football coaching).

Activities **galore...**

Well equipped campsites might offer any of the following activities: pony riding, cycling, minigolf for the younger ones. For slightly older children there might be tennis, archery and watersports. And that's before you start talking about the impressive aqua parks springing up on many continental campsites, complete with waterslides, lagoons, wave machines and huge waterchutes.

Join the **club**

Children love camping, and campsites love children. That's why many campsites run their own children's clubs, often in high season. Most good ones will be multilingual (though language barriers often seem not to exist among children). Clubs may be free, depending on what's on offer and activities may range from organised treasure hunts, group activities like painting, crafts, nature rambles and ball games. Some even arrange kids' talent shows.

That's **entertainment**

Many campsites lay on organised entertainment, especially in high season, and often this is free of charge. It might be local music evenings, a family talent show or disco, fancy dress competition or a magic show. Good campsites will ensure appropriate events for different age groups. Of course, such entertainment may not be on your wish list: if so, a useful rule of thumb is that the larger the campsite, the more likely it is that it will offer regular organised entertainment in high season.

Life through
a **child's eye**

For many, part of the appeal of camping is that it gives a different perspective on the mundane aspects of everyday life. Children generally view this as an adventure, and for younger children just beginning to stretch their wings, a campsite provides a perfect environment (safe, friendly) to enjoy such adventures.

So, whether holidaying in the UK or abroad, the simple task of buying bread from the campsite shop often becomes a fun part of the holiday for the intrepid seven year old. Handing over some coins, saying 'Hello' or 'Bonjour' and returning to base without nibbling too much is often a small milestone in the early years.

Fresh **experiences**

When camping, so much is new and unfamiliar. There's always the excitement and anticipation of arriving at your site and choosing your pitch – home for the holiday. Setting up camp, meeting the neighbours and getting organised is always fun. Unpacking all the outdoor games and trying to play everything at once, then clamouring for a swim, or an ice cream... probably both.

The washing up ritual is peculiar to camping. While at home this is no more than routine drudgery of everyday life, but on a campsite somehow it can become part of a family bonding team building exercise, enlivened by banter at the sinks with total strangers. Kids seem to love it!

Evenings may be an opportunity to enjoy some organised entertainment: depending on location, this might be Breton bagpipes, a Scottish dancing demonstration, a cheesy song and dance routine or a mock talent show. Unlikely to be highbrow culture but the youngsters generally enjoy the novelty of it all, being outdoors under the stars (hopefully), running around until later than usual.

And when it's time to turn in, the chances are the younger children will be sleepy and ready to drop off. But the notion of sliding into a comfy sleeping bag always seems more fun than just another bed.

Enjoy...!

Whether you're an 'old hand' or are contemplating your first trip, a regular reader of our Guides or a new 'convert', we wish you well in your travels and hope we have been able to help in some way. We are, of course, also out and about ourselves, visiting sites, talking to owners and readers, and generally checking on standards and new developments. We hope to bump into you!

Wishing you thoroughly enjoyable camping and caravanning in 2012 – favoured by good weather of course!

The Alan Rogers Team

Q&**A**

Do campsites have WiFi?
Many do, usually for a charge.

My children don't speak French/other languages!
Don't worry, language barriers are not so important for the under 12s. Children of all nationalities seem to make friends and happily run around on a campsite.

Are campsite discos suitable for younger children?
Well run campsites will ensure these are age-restricted, with sensible and fair end-times. Some are for 'all the family' while others are definitely for older teenagers.

How safe are campsites for young children?
Safety is a big issue on all campsites and good campsites will have rules and procedures in place to enforce this. For example, rules may apply to usage of washblocks or the play area. While generally speaking children can run around safely, usual parental responsibilities still apply.

Are babysitting and crèche facilities available?
Some sites do offer babysitting (likely to depend on willing summer staff). Crèche services are less common, though children's clubs run by the campsite tend to fulfil such needs. Of course, these will vary widely.

Do campsites provide baby equipment?
Most campsites can provide a 'baby pack' (cot and highchair) but this is mostly for the accommodation market (e.g. mobile homes).

SPAIN – Sant Pere Pescador

Camping Las Dunas

Ctra San Marti - Sant Pere, E-17470 Sant Pere Pescador (Girona)
t: **972 521 717** e: **info@campinglasdunas.com**
alanrogers.com/ES80400 www.campinglasdunas.com

Accommodation: ☑ Pitch ☑ Mobile home/chalet ☐ Hotel/B&B ☐ Apartment

Las Dunas is an extremely large, impressive and well organised resort style site with
many on-site activities and an ongoing programme of improvements. It has direct
access to a superb sandy beach that stretches along the site for nearly a kilometre with
a windsurfing school and beach bar. There is also a much used, huge swimming pool,
plus a large double pool for children. Las Dunas is very large, with 1,700 individual
hedged pitches (1,479 for tourers) of around 100 sq.m. laid out on flat ground in long,
regular parallel rows. All have electricity (6/10A) and 180 also have water and drainage.
Shade is available in some parts of the site. Pitches are usually available, even in the
main season. Much effort has gone into planting palms and new trees here and the
results are very attractive. The large restaurant and bar have spacious terraces
overlooking the swimming pools or you can enjoy a very pleasant, more secluded,
cavern style pub. A magnificent disco club is close by in a soundproofed building.

You might like to know
Excellent entertainment (for children and
adults alike) is organised daily in peak season,
including flamenco music and spectacular
magic shows.

- ☑ Multilingual children's club – pre-school
- ☑ Multilingual children's club – 5-10 year olds
- ☑ Multilingual children's club – 10-14 year olds
- ☑ Creative crafts
- ☐ Bicycle hire for children
- ☑ Facilities for children in wash blocks
- ☑ Children's pool
- ☑ Children's play area
- ☐ Crèche and/or babysitting
- ☑ Local information of interest
  for children

Facilities: Five excellent large toilet blocks
(resident cleaners 07.00-21.00). British style
toilets but no seats, controllable hot showers
and washbasins in cabins. Excellent facilities
for youngsters, babies and disabled campers.
Laundry facilities. Motorcaravan services.
Extensive supermarket, boutique and other
shops. Large bar with terrace. Large restaurant.
Takeaway. Ice cream parlour. Beach bar
(high season). Disco club. Swimming pools.
Playgrounds. Tennis. Archery. Minigolf.
Sailing/windsurfing school and watersports.
Activity programme, partly in English (15/6-31/8).
Exchange facilities. ATM. WiFi. Dogs taken in
one section. Torches required in some areas.
Off site: Resort of L'Escala 5 km. Riding and boat
launching 5 km. Water park 10 km. Golf 30 km.

Open: 19 May - 2 September.

Directions: From A7/E15 autostrada take exit
5 towards L'Escala on GI 623. Turn north 2 km.
before L'Escala towards Sant Marti d'Ampúrias.
Site well signed. GPS: 42.16098, 3.13478

Charges guide

Per unit incl. 2 persons and electricity	€ 21,00 - € 59,20
extra person	€ 3,50 - € 5,75
child (3-10 yrs)	€ 3,00 - € 3,25

Camping Internacional de Calonge

Ctra San Feliu/Guixols - Palamós km 7.6, E-17251 Calonge (Girona)
t: 972 651 233   e: info@intercalonge.com
alanrogers.com/ES81300   www.intercalonge.com

Accommodation: ☑Pitch ☑Mobile home/chalet ☐ Hotel/B&B ☐ Apartment

This spacious, well laid out site has access to a fine beach via a footbridge over the coast road, or you can take the little road train as the site is on very sloping ground. Calonge is a family site with two good sized pools on different levels, a paddling pool and large sunbathing areas. A great restaurant, bar and snack bar are by the pool. The site's 793 pitches are on terraces and all have electricity (5A), with 84 being fully serviced. The pitches are set on attractively landscaped terraces (access to some may be challenging). There is good shade from the tall pine trees and some views of the sea through the foliage. The views from the upper levels are taken by a tour operator and mobile home pitches. The pools are overlooked by the restaurant terraces. A nature area within the site is used for walks and picnics. A separate area within the site is set aside for visitors with dogs (including a dog shower!) The beach is accessed over the main road by 100 steps and is shared with another campsite (ES81400).

You might like to know

There is a great variety of activities on offer here, including windsurfing, snorkeling and golf, for all ages from the youngest to the oldest.

- ☐ Multilingual children's club – pre-school
- ☑ Multilingual children's club – 5-10 year olds
- ☑ Multilingual children's club – 10-14 year olds
- ☑ Creative crafts
- ☑ Bicycle hire for children
- ☑ Facilities for children in wash blocks
- ☑ Children's pool
- ☑ Children's play area
- ☐ Crèche and/or babysitting
- ☑ Local information of interest for children

Facilities: Both new and renovated sanitary blocks include some washbasins in cabins. No toilet seats. One block is heated in winter. Laundry facilities. Motorcaravan services. Gas supplies. Shop (26/3-30/10), Restaurant (1/2-31/12). Bar, patio bar with pizzas and takeaway (27/3-24/10, then weekends). Swimming pools (26/3-16/10). Playground. Electronic games. Disco two nights a week (but not late). Bicycle hire. Tennis. Hairdresser. ATM. WiFi. Torches necessary in some areas. Road train from the bottom of the site to the top in high season. Off site: Bus at the gate. Fishing 300 m. Supermarket 500 m. Golf 3 km. Riding 10 km.

Open: All year.

Directions: Site is on the inland side of the coast road between Palamós and Platja d'Aro. Take the C31 south to the 661 at Calonge. At Calonge follow signs to the C253 towards Platja d'Aro and on to site which is well signed. GPS: 41.83333, 3.08417

Charges guide

Per unit incl. 2 persons and electricity	€ 19,65 - € 44,65
extra person	€ 3,65 - € 7,85
child (3-10 yrs)	€ 1,85 - € 4,40

No credit cards.

SPAIN – Salou

Camping Resort Sangulí Salou

Prolongacion Calle, Apdo 123, E-43840 Salou (Tarragona)
t: 977 381 641   e: mail@sanguli.es
alanrogers.com/ES84800   www.sanguli.es

Accommodation: ☑ Pitch ☑ Mobile home/chalet ☐ Hotel/B&B ☐ Apartment

Sangulí is a superb site boasting excellent pools and entertainment for the whole family. Owned, developed and managed by a local Spanish family, it provides for all the family with everything open when the site is open. There are 1,067 pitches of varying size (75-100 sq.m) and all have electricity. Mobile homes occupy 58 pitches and there are fully equipped bungalows on 147. A wonderful selection of trees, palms and shrubs provides natural shade and an ideal space for children to play. The good sandy beach is little more than 100 metres across the coast road and a small railway crossing. Although large, Sangulí has a pleasant, open feel and maintains a quality family atmosphere due to the efforts of the very keen and efficient staff. Located on the promenade near the centre of Salou, the site can offer the attractions of a busy resort while still being private and it is only 3 km. from Port Aventura. This is a large, professional site providing something for all the family, but still providing peace and quiet for those looking for it.

You might like to know
Special services for children include the Mini Club with its mascot, Guli, sports competitions and children's shows. Loan of cots. Children's menu, high chair and bib etc. in the restaurant.

- ☐ Multilingual children's club – pre-school
- ☑ Multilingual children's club – 5-10 year olds
- ☑ Multilingual children's club – 10-14 year olds
- ☑ Creative crafts
- ☐ Bicycle hire for children
- ☑ Facilities for children in wash blocks
- ☑ Children's pool
- ☑ Children's play area
- ☐ Crèche and/or babysitting
- ☑ Local information of interest for children

Facilities: The six sanitary blocks are constantly cleaned and are always exceptional, including many individual cabins with en-suite facilities. Improvements are made each year. Some blocks have excellent facilities for babies. Launderette with service. Motorcaravan services. Car wash (charged). Gas supplies. Snack bars. Indoor and outdoor restaurants with takeaway. Swimming pools. Fitness centre. Sports complex. Fitness room (charged). Playgrounds including adventure play area. Miniclub. Minigolf. Multiple Internet options including WiFi. Security bracelets. Well equipped medical centre. Off site: Bus at gate. Fishing and bicycle hire 100 m. Riding 3 km. Port Aventura 4 km. Resort entertainment. Golf 6 km.

Open: 19 March - 1 November.

Directions: On west side of Salou about 1 km. from the centre, site is well signed from the coast road to Cambrils and from the other town approaches. GPS: 41.075, 1.116

Charges guide

Per unit incl. 2 persons and electricity	€ 27,00 - € 71,00
extra person	€ 6,00
child (4-12 yrs)	€ 4,00

Marjal Costa Blanca Eco Resort

AP7. Salida 730 (Catral-San Felipe Neri), E-03330 Crevillente (Alacant)
t: 965 484 945 e: camping@marjalcostablanca.com
alanrogers.com/ES87435 www.marjalcostablanca.com

Accommodation: ☑ Pitch ☑ Mobile home/chalet ☐ Hotel/B&B ☐ Apartment

Marjal Costa Blanca is a brand new site which is opening in December 2011. We will undertake a full inspection in 2012. There will be 1,500 pitches here, ranging in size from 90–180 sq.m. All pitches will have electricity, water and drainage. A number of new mobile homes will also be available. The site is a major new initiative and is sure to become one of the most modern and best equipped campsites in Spain. Leisure amenities will include a tropically themed swimming pool complex and a state-of-the-art wellness centre. The site's principal restaurant, Marjal Plaza, is open all year and, during summer months, will feature a buffet with fresh, local produce. The site has been developed along very strict environmental guidelines. More than 7,000 mulberry trees have been planted and every effort has been made to conserve resources and use sustainable materials. There's plenty going in peak season, including a lively children's club, which will be led by the site's mascot, 'Marjalita'.

Special offers
Kids go free during 2012 (4-12 years).

You might like to know
A great choice for a sunny holiday. The average temperature in this region is 20ºC and there are well over 300 sunny days a year.

☑ Multilingual children's club – pre-school
☑ Multilingual children's club – 5-10 year olds
☑ Multilingual children's club – 10-14 year olds
☑ Creative crafts
☐ Bicycle hire for children
☑ Facilities for children in wash blocks
☑ Children's pool
☑ Children's play area
☑ Crèche and/or babysitting
☑ Local information of interest for children

Facilities: Supermarket. Bar, snack bar, restaurant and takeaway food. Tropical swimming pool complex. Play areas. Wellness centre. Hairdresser. Library. Tennis. Football. Entertainment and activity programme. Mobile homes and chalets to rent. Business centre. Car hire service. Pet care facilities. Tourist information. Off site: Nearest beach 15 km. El Honda nature reserve. Terra Mitica theme park.

Open: All year.

Directions: Take the southbound A7 coastal motorway until you reach the fork near Elche- Crevillente. Continue on AP7 towards Cartagena and then take exit 730 (Catral) and follow signs to the site.
GPS: 38.177901, -0.809504

Charges guide

Per unit incl. 2 persons and electricity (plus meter)	€ 25,00 - € 32,00
extra person	€ 4,00
child (4-12 yrs)	€ 3,00
dog	€ 1,50

SPAIN – Noja

Camping Playa Joyel

Playa de Ris, E-39180 Noja (Cantabria)
t: **942 630 081** e: **playajoyel@telefonica.net**
alanrogers.com/ES90000 www.playajoyel.com

Accommodation: ☑Pitch ☑Mobile home/chalet ☐ Hotel/B&B ☐ Apartment

This very attractive holiday and touring site is some 40 kilometres from Santander and 80 kilometres from Bilbao. It is a busy, high quality, comprehensively equipped site by a superb beach providing 1,000 well shaded, marked and numbered pitches with 6A electricity available. These include 80 large pitches of 100 sq.m. Some 250 pitches are occupied by tour operators or seasonal units. This well managed site has a lot to offer for family holidays with much going on in high season when it gets crowded. The swimming pool complex (with lifeguard) is free to campers and the superb beaches are cleaned daily mid June to mid September. Two beach exits lead to the main beach where there are some undertows, or if you turn left you will find a reasonably placid estuary. An unusual feature here is the nature park within the site boundary which has a selection of animals to see. This overlooks a protected area of marsh where European birds spend the winter.

You might like to know
Why not visit Santillana del Mar, a beautiful old town with winding medieval streets?

☑ Multilingual children's club – pre-school
☑ Multilingual children's club – 5-10 year olds
☑ Multilingual children's club – 10-14 year olds
☑ Creative crafts
☐ Bicycle hire for children
☑ Facilities for children in wash blocks
☑ Children's pool
☑ Children's play area
☐ Crèche and/or babysitting
☐ Local information of interest for children

Facilities: Six excellent, spacious and fully equipped toilet blocks include baby baths. Large laundry. Motorcaravan services. Gas supplies. Freezer service. Supermarket (all season). General shop. Kiosk. Restaurant and takeaway (1/7-31/8). Bar and snacks (all season). Swimming pools, bathing caps compulsory (20/5-15/9). Entertainment. Soundproofed pub/disco (July/Aug). Gym park. Tennis. Playground. Riding. Fishing. Nature animal park. Hairdresser (July/Aug). Medical centre. Torches necessary in some areas. Animals are not accepted. Off site: Bicycle hire. Sports complex with indoor pool 1 km. Sailing and boat launching 10 km. Riding and golf 20 km.

Open: 15 April - 1 October.

Directions: From A8 (Bilbao - Santander) take km. 185 exit and N634 towards Beranga. Almost immediately turn right on CA147 to Noja. In 10 km. turn left at multiple campsite signs and go through town. At beach follow signs to site. GPS: 43.48948, -3.53700

Charges guide

Per unit incl. 2 persons and electricity	€ 28,20 - € 47,40
extra person	€ 4,40 - € 6,70
child (3-9 yrs)	€ 3,10 - € 5,00

PORTUGAL – Odemira

Zmar-Eco Camping Resort

Herdade a de Mateus E.N. 393/1, San Salvador, P-7630 Odemira (Beja)
t: **707 200 626** e: **info@zmar.eu**
alanrogers.com/PO8175 www.zmar.eu

Accommodation: ☑ Pitch ☑ Mobile home/chalet ☐ Hotel/B&B ☐ Apartment

Zmar is an exciting new project which should be fully open this year. The site is located near Zambujeira do Mar, on the Alentejo coast. This is a highly ambitious initiative developed along very strict environmental lines. For example, renewable resources such as locally harvested timber and recycled plastic are used wherever possible and solar energy is used whenever practicable. Public indoor spaces have no air conditioning, but there is adequate cooling through underfloor ventilation and electric fans where possible. Pitches are 100 sq.m. and benefit from artificial shade. Caravans and wood-clad mobile homes are also available for rent. The swimming pool complex features a large outdoor pool and an indoor pool area with a wave machine and a wellness centre. The very large and innovative children's play park has climbing nets, labyrinths and caves. There is also a children's farm and a large play house. For adults, many sporting amenities will be available around the resort's 81 hectare park.

You might like to know
Zmar is a new concept in eco-tourism and many children's activities reflect these concerns.

☐ Multilingual children's club – pre-school
☑ Multilingual children's club – 5-10 year olds
☑ Multilingual children's club – 10-14 year olds
☑ Creative crafts
☑ Bicycle hire for children
☑ Facilities for children in wash blocks
☑ Children's pool
☑ Children's play area
☑ Crèche and/or babysitting
☑ Local information of interest for children

Facilities: Eight toilet blocks provide comprehensive facilities including those for children and disabled visitors. Bar. Restaurant. Crêperie. Takeaway food. Large supermarket. Swimming pool. Covered pool. Wellness centre. Sports field. Games room. Play area, farm and play house. Tennis. Bicycle hire. Activity and entertainment programme. Mobile homes and caravans for rent. Caravan repair and servicing. The site's own debit card system is used for payment at all facilities. Off site: Vicentina coast and the Alentejo natural park. Sines (birthplace of Vasco de Gama). Cycle and walking tracks. Sea fishing.

Open: All year.

Directions: From the N120 from Odemira to Lagos, at roundabout in the centre of Portas de Transval turn towards Milfontes. Take turn to Cabo Sardão and then Zambujeira do Mar. Site is on the left. GPS: 37.60422, -8.73142

Charges guide

Per unit incl. up to 4 persons and electricity	€ 20,00 - € 50,00
extra person	€ 5,00 - € 10,00
child (4-12 yrs)	€ 5,00

PORTUGAL – Lagos

Camping Turiscampo

N125, Espiche, Luz, P-8600 Lagos (Faro)
t: 282 789 265 e: info@turiscampo.com
alanrogers.com/PO8202 www.turiscampo.com

Accommodation: ☑Pitch ☑Mobile home/chalet ☐ Hotel/B&B ☐ Apartment

This good quality site has been thoughtfully refurbished and updated since it was purchased by the friendly Coll family, who are known to us from their previous Spanish site. The site provides 206 pitches for touring units, mainly in rows of terraces, all with electricity (6/10A) and some with shade. Twelve pitches have water and waste water. The pitches vary in size (70-120 sq.m). The upper areas of the site are mainly used for bungalow accommodation (and are generally separate from the touring areas). A new, elevated Californian style pool plus a children's pool have been constructed. The supporting structure is a clever water cascade and surround, and a large sun lounger area on astroturf. One side of the pool area is open to the road. The restaurant/bar has been tastefully refurbished and Roberto and his staff are delighted to use their excellent English, providing good fare at most reasonable prices. The sea is 2 km. and the city of Lagos 4 km. This is a very good site for families and for 'snowbirds' to over-winter.

You might like to know

Children can learn the basics of Tai Chi with our fully-qualified instructors.

☐ Multilingual children's club – pre-school
☑ Multilingual children's club – 5-10 year olds
☑ Multilingual children's club – 10-14 year olds
☑ Creative crafts
☐ Bicycle hire for children
☑ Facilities for children in wash blocks
☑ Children's pool
☑ Children's play area
☐ Crèche and/or babysitting
☑ Local information of interest for children

Facilities: Four toilet blocks are well located around the site. Two have been refurbished, two are new and contain modern facilities for disabled campers. Hot water throughout. Facilities for children. Washing machines. Shop. Gas supplies. Restaurant/bar. Swimming pool (Mar-Oct) with two terraces. Bicycle hire. Entertainment in high season on the bar terrace. Two children's playgrounds. Adult art workshops. Aqua gymnastics. Miniclub (5-12 yrs) in season. Boules. Archery. Sports field. Cable TV. Internet. WiFi on payment. Off site: Bus to Lagos and other towns from Praia da Luz village 1.5 km. Fishing and beach 2 km. Golf 4 km. Sailing and boat launching 5 km. Riding 10 km.

Open: All year.

Directions: Take exit 1 from the N125 Lagos - Vila do Bispo. The impressive entrance is about 3 km. on the right. GPS: 37.10111, -8.73278

Charges guide

Per unit incl. 2 persons and electricity	€ 16,20 - € 28,83
extra person	€ 3,28 - € 6,56
child (3-10 yrs)	€ 1,77 - € 3,28
dog	€ 1,01

Centro Vacanze Pra' Delle Torri

P.O. Box 176, Via Altanea 201, I-30021 Caorle (Veneto)
t: **042 129 9063** e: **info@pradelletorri.it**
alanrogers.com/IT60030 www.pradelletorri.it

Accommodation: ☑Pitch ☑Mobile home/chalet ☑Hotel/B&B ☐ Apartment

Pra' Delle Torri is a superb Italian Adriatic site which has just about everything! Pitches for camping, hotel, accommodation to rent and two very large, well equipped pool complexes, which may be rated among the best in the country. There is also a full size golf course. Of the 1,500 pitches, 888 are for touring and are arranged in zones, with 5-10A electricity and shade. There is an amazing choice of good restaurants, bars and shops arranged around an attractive square. Although a large site, there is a great atmosphere here that families will enjoy. The fabulous lagoon pool complex with islands, slides and sunbathing areas is the site's crowning glory plus indoor (Olympic size) and outdoor laned pools. Other amenities include a grassy area for ball games, a good playground, a children's car track, and a whole range of sports and entertainment programmes, along with a medical centre, skincare and other therapies. The site has its own sandy beach and Porto Santa, Margherita and Caorle are nearby.

You might like to know
The aqua park here is one of the largest in Italy. There's so much to do that you won't want to leave the site!

- ☑ Multilingual children's club – pre-school
- ☑ Multilingual children's club – 5-10 year olds
- ☑ Multilingual children's club – 10-14 year olds
- ☑ Creative crafts
- ☑ Bicycle hire for children
- ☑ Facilities for children in wash blocks
- ☑ Children's pool
- ☑ Children's play area
- ☑ Crèche and/or babysitting
- ☑ Local information of interest for children

Facilities: Sixteen high quality toilet blocks with excellent facilities including very attractive 'junior stations'. Units for disabled visitors. Laundry. Motorcaravan service point. Large supermarket and wide range of shops, restaurants, bars and takeaways. Indoor and outdoor pools. Tennis. Minigolf. Fishing. Watersports. Archery. Fitness programmes and keep fit track. Diving. Crèche and supervised play area. Bowls. Mountain bike track. Wide range of organised sports and entertainment. Road train to town in high season. Dogs are not accepted. Off site: Riding 3 km. Beach fishing. Tours and excursions.

Open: 16 April - 1 October.

Directions: From A4 Venice - Trieste motorway leave at exit for Sto Stino di Livenze and follow signs to Caorle then Sta Margherita and signs to site. GPS: 45.57312, 12.81248

Charges guide

Per unit incl. 2 persons and electricity	€ 16,40 - € 62,80
extra person	€ 4,20 - € 9,90
child (2-5 yrs)	free - € 7,00
child (6-12 yrs)	€ 1,00 - € 8,20

Camping Union Lido Vacanze

Via Fausta 258, I-30013 Cavallino-Treporti (Veneto)
t: **041 257 5111** e: **info@unionlido.com**
alanrogers.com/IT60200 www.unionlido.com

Accommodation: ☑Pitch ☑Mobile home/chalet ☑Hotel/B&B ☑Apartment

This amazing site is very large, offering everything a camper could wish for. It is extremely well organised and it has been said to set the standard that others follow. It lies right beside the sea with direct access to a 1.2 km. long, broad sandy beach which shelves very gradually and provides very safe bathing (there are lifeguards). The site itself is regularly laid out with parallel access roads under a covering of poplars, pine and other trees providing good shade. There are 2,222 pitches for touring units, all with 6/10A electricity and 1,777 also have water and drainage. You really would not need to leave this site – everything is here, including a sophisticated wellness centre. There are two aqua parks, one with fine sandy beaches (a first in Europe). A heated pool for hotel and apartment guests is open to others on payment. A huge selection of sports is offered and entertainment and fitness programmes are organised in season. Union Lido is above all an orderly and clean site. A member of Leading Campings Group.

You might like to know

One of Europe's largest sites, looking straight out to the Adriatic with a long private beach (1,200 metres), Union Lido is a top quality holiday centre with a wide range of amenities.

- ☑ Multilingual children's club – pre-school
- ☑ Multilingual children's club – 5-10 year olds
- ☑ Multilingual children's club – 10-14 year olds
- ☑ Creative crafts
- ☑ Bicycle hire for children
- ☑ Facilities for children in wash blocks
- ☑ Children's pool
- ☑ Children's play area
- ☐ Crèche and/or babysitting
- ☑ Local information of interest for children

Facilities: Fourteen well kept, fully equipped toilet blocks which open and close progressively during the season; 11 have facilities for disabled visitors. Launderette. Motorcaravan service points. Gas supplies. Comprehensive shopping areas set around a pleasant piazza (all open till late). Eight restaurants plus 11 pleasant and lively bars. Impressive aqua parks (all season). Tennis. Riding. Minigolf. Skating. Bicycle hire. Archery. Golf academy. Diving centre and school. Windsurfing school in season. Boat excursions. Recreational events. Church service in English in July/Aug. Hairdressers. Internet cafés. ATM. Dogs are not accepted. Off site: Boat launching 3.5 km. Aqualandia (special rates).

Open: 22 April - 25 September (with all services).

Directions: From Venice - Trieste autostrada leave at exit for airport or Quarto d'Altino and follow signs first for Jesolo and then Punta Sabbioni, and site will be seen just after Cavallino on the left. GPS: 45.467883, 12.530367

Charges guide

Per unit incl. 2 persons and electricity	€ 25,40 - € 60,00
extra person	€ 6,60 - € 10,50
child (6-11 yrs)	€ 5,20 - € 8,80
child (1-5 yrs)	€ 3,70 - € 7,10

Camping Marina di Venezia

Via Montello 6, I-30013 Punta Sabbioni (Veneto)
t: 041 530 2511   e: camping@marinadivenezia.it
alanrogers.com/IT60450   www.marinadivenezia.it

Accommodation: ☑ Pitch ☑ Mobile home/chalet ☐ Hotel/B&B ☐ Apartment

This is a very large site (2,853 pitches) with much the same atmosphere as many other large sites along this appealing stretch of coastline. Marina di Venezia, however, has the advantage of being within walking distance of the ferry to Venice. It will appeal particularly to those who enjoy an extensive range of entertainment and activities, and a lively atmosphere. Individual pitches are marked out on sandy or grassy ground, most separated by trees or hedges. They are of an average size for the region (around 80 sq.m) and all are equipped with electricity and water. The site's excellent sandy each is one of the widest along this stretch of coast and has five pleasant beach bars. The main pool is Olympic size and there is also a very large children's pool adjacent. The magnificent Aqua Marina Park swimming pool complex is now open and offers amazing amenities (free to all campers). This is a well run site with committed management and staff.

You might like to know

There's plenty to keep the family entertained – Gommaland, minigolf, baby-cars, bumper-boats, and in high season football school, sports tournaments, archery, aquagym, ballet school and baby dance.

☐ Multilingual children's club – pre-school
☑ Multilingual children's club – 5-10 year olds
☑ Multilingual children's club – 10-14 year olds
☑ Creative crafts
☑ Bicycle hire for children
☑ Facilities for children in wash blocks
☑ Children's pool
☑ Children's play area
☐ Crèche and/or babysitting
☑ Local information of interest for children

Facilities: Ten modern toilet blocks (two recently replaced by a new one) are maintained to a high standard with good hot showers and a reasonable proportion of British style toilets. Good provision for disabled visitors. Washing machines and dryers. Range of shops. Several bars, restaurants and takeaways. Swimming pool complex with slides and flumes. Several play areas. Tennis. Windsurf and catamaran hire. Kite hire. Wide range of organised entertainment. WiFi internet access in all bars and cafés. Church. Special area and facilities for dog owners.

Open: 16 April - 30 September.

Directions: From A4 motorway, take Jesolo exit. After Jesolo continue towards Punta Sabbioni. Site is clearly signed to the left towards the end of this road, close to the Venice ferries. GPS: 45.43750, 12.43805

Charges guide

Per unit incl. 2 persons and electricity	€ 19,80 - € 47,60
extra person	€ 4,40 - € 9,70
child (2-5 yrs) and senior (60+)	€ 3,70 - € 7,80
dog	€ 1,10 - € 3,30

Camping Village Oasi

Via A Barbarigo 147, I-30015 Sottomarina di Chioggia (Veneto)
t: 041 554 1145   e: info@campingoasi.com
alanrogers.com/IT60540   www.campingoasi.com

Accommodation: ☑Pitch ☑Mobile home/chalet   ☐ Hotel/B&B ☐ Apartment

Camping Oasi is a traditional, friendly, family site where many Italian families return for the summer – you could certainly practise your Italian language skills here. The Tiozzi family will make you feel very welcome. The flat, grass pitches for tourers are in separate areas from the permanent units, some being near the playground and football area. Varying in size (65-80 sq.m) with a choice of shade or sun, all have 6A electricity, 100 have water and drainage. There is a harbour wall walk to the private soft sand beach where a second bar and restaurant provides drinks, snacks and meals. The touring pitches are near this beach access. The site has two restaurants – try the seafood, it is excellent! An entertainment team works with children through the day in high season, culminating in a show outside the restaurant in the evening. We recommend a bicycle trip to the ancient fishing city of Choggia. It resembles a mini-Venice with its narrow streets and canals. By night it has a very special charm.

You might like to know

Sottomarina's beaches are famous for their water quality and pristine fine sand – perfect for a lazy afternoon.

- ☑ Multilingual children's club – pre-school
- ☑ Multilingual children's club – 5-10 year olds
- ☑ Multilingual children's club – 10-14 year olds
- ☑ Creative crafts
- ☐ Bicycle hire for children
- ☑ Facilities for children in wash blocks
- ☑ Children's pool
- ☑ Children's play area
- ☐ Crèche and/or babysitting
- ☑ Local information of interest for children

Facilities: Two good sanitary blocks with mostly British style toilets and free hot showers. There are good facilities for disabled visitors and for children and babies (both some way from the furthest touring pitches). Pleasant swimming pool and paddling pool with flumes (a hoist is available allowing easier access for disabled visitors into the swimming pool). Adventure play area. Multisport pitch. Tennis. Bicycle hire. Riding. Watersports. Fishing. WiFi (charged). Communal barbecue area. Off site: Historical city of Chioggia. ATM 2 km.

Open: 25 March - 30 September.

Directions: Site is off the S309 south of Chioggia. Follow signs to Sottomarina, crossing Laguna del Lusenzo, then look for site signs. Site off this road (Viale Mediterranneo) to the right. Site is last along this narrow road. GPS: 45.18148, 12.30755

Charges guide

Per unit incl. 2 persons and electricity	€ 20,10 - € 35,10
extra person	€ 5,40 - € 8,30
child (1-5 yrs)	€ 2,60 - € 4,40
dog	€ 2,70 - € 3,70

Camping Seiser Alm

Saint Konstantin 16, I-39050 Völs am Schlern (Trentino - Alto Adige)
t: 047 170 6459   e: info@camping-seiseralm.com
alanrogers.com/IT62040   www.camping-seiseralm.com

Accommodation: ☑ Pitch ☑ Mobile home/chalet   ☐ Hotel/B&B ☑ Apartment

What an amazing experience awaits you at Seiser Alm! Elisabeth and Erhard Mahlknecht have created a superb site in the magnificent Südtirol region of the Dolomite mountains. Towering peaks provide a magnificent backdrop when you dine in the charming, traditional style restaurant on the upper terrace. Here you will also find the bar, shop and reception. The 150 touring pitches are of a very high standard with 16A electricity supply, 120 with gas, water, drainage and satellite connections. Guests were delighted with the site when we visited, many coming to walk or cycle, some just to enjoy the surroundings. There are countless things to see and do here. Local buses and cable cars provide an excellent service for summer visitors and skiers alike (discounts are available). In keeping with the natural setting, the majority of the luxury facilities are set into the hillside. Elisabeth's designs incorporating Grimm fairy tales are tastefully developed in the superb children's bathrooms that are in a magic forest setting complete with blue sky, giant mushroom and elves!

You might like to know

A family play park with an enclosure of tame rabbits is at the lower part of the site where goats also roam.

☐ Multilingual children's club – pre-school
☑ Multilingual children's club – 5-10 year olds
☑ Multilingual children's club – 10-14 year olds
☑ Creative crafts
☐ Bicycle hire for children
☑ Facilities for children in wash blocks
☐ Children's pool
☑ Children's play area
☑ Crèche and/or babysitting
☑ Local information of interest for children

Facilities: One luxury underground block is in the centre of the site. 16 private units are available. Excellent facilities for disabled visitors. Fairy tale facilities for children. Infrared sensors, underfloor heating and gently curved floors to prevent slippery surfaces. Constant fresh air ventilation. Washing machines and large drying room. Sauna. Supermarket. Quality restaurant and bar with terrace. Entertainment programme. Miniclub. Children's adventure park and play room. Special rooms for ski equipment. WiFi (charged). Apartments and mobile homes for rent.

Open: All year excl. 2 November - 20 December.

Directions: Site is east of Bolzano. From the A22-E45 take Bolzano Nord exit. Take road for Prato Isarco/Blumau, then road for Fie/Völs. Take care as the split in the road is sudden and if you miss the left fork as you enter a tunnel (Altopiano dello Sciliar/Schlerngebiet) you will pay a heavy price in extra kilometres. Enjoy the climb to Völs am Schlern and site is well signed.
GPS: 46.53344, 11.53335.

Charges guide

per unit incl. 2 persons	€ 17,30 - € 43,50
extra person	€ 6,90 - € 9,50
child (2-16 yrs)	€ 3,60 - € 7,70
electricity (per kWh)	€ 0,60

ITALY – Fucine di Ossana

Camping Cevedale

Via di Sotto Pila 4, I-38026 Fucine di Ossana (Trentino - Alto Adige)
t: **046 375 1630** e: **info@campingcevedale.it**
alanrogers.com/IT62110 www.campingcevedale.it

Accommodation: ☑Pitch ☐ Mobile home/chalet ☐ Hotel/B&B ☐ Apartment

Nestled under a castle and close to a tiny village, Camping Cevedale has a European atmosphere with very little English spoken, except by Maura, who runs the site. The 197 pitches are grouped in two areas on either side of a fast flowing river (fenced) which can be noisy. The touring pitches, all with electricity (only 2A), are shaded, on grass and slope somewhat; they are in various areas among the well kept seasonal caravans. Some campers come here every holiday and most have built little wooden chalets next to their caravans. This area is known for skiing in winter, rafting, adventure sports, mountain bike riding and trekking. Adventure sport courses are arranged by the management, and access to this kind of activity is one of the site's strengths.

Special offers
Children under 8 go free. Winter ski offer: 1 child goes free when accompanied by a paying adult. Included in the price: hot water in the showers, 2A electricity, camper service and ski bus.

You might like to know
Ski resorts are just 15 minutes away by free ski bus, which stops in front of the campsite. The campsite is on the 30 km. Val di Sole cycling route, in Parco dello Stevio, with miles of cycling for all ages and abilities.

☐ Multilingual children's club – pre-school
☑ Multilingual children's club – 5-10 year olds
☑ Multilingual children's club – 10-14 year olds
☑ Creative crafts
☑ Bicycle hire for children
☑ Facilities for children in wash blocks
☐ Children's pool
☑ Children's play area
☐ Crèche and/or babysitting
☑ Local information of interest for children

Facilities: Two sanitary blocks with mainly Turkish style toilets are well maintained, modern and spotlessly clean. They include hot water for showers and basins, heating in winter, washing machine and dryer. Small shop. Pleasant bar which serves snacks. Play area with tables and barbecues. Internet access. WiFi throughout (free). Adventure sport courses arranged. Bicycle hire. Dogs are not accepted. Off site: Riding 3 km. Skiing 10 km. Trekking, cycling, climbing, rope courses, abseiling, canyoning, rafting, fishing nearby.

Open: All year.

Directions: Fucine is 50 km. northwest of Trento. From the A22 (Brenner - Modena) take exit for S. Michele, north of Trento, then SS43 north for 43 km. to Cles. Turn east on the SS42 for 26 km. to Fucine. Continue through village and turn south on SP202 (Ossana). Follow signs for campsite (ignore any alternative suggestions from sat nav!). The entrance is next to the bridge just below the castle. GPS: 46.30834, 10.73361

Charges guide

Per unit incl. 2 persons and electricity	€ 25,00 - € 32,00
extra person	€ 8,00 - € 9,00
child (0-8 yrs)	€ 6,00 - € 7,00

Camping Villaggio dei Fiori

Via Tiro a Volo 3, I-18038 San Remo (Ligúria)
t: **018 466 0635** e: **info@villaggiodeifiori.it**
alanrogers.com/IT64010 www.villaggiodeifiori.it

Accommodation: ☑Pitch ☑Mobile home/chalet ☐ Hotel/B&B ☐ Apartment

Open all year round, this open and spacious site has high standards and is ideal for exploring the Italian Riviera or for just relaxing by the enjoyable, filtered sea water pools. Unusually, all the pitch areas at the site are totally paved and there are some extremely large pitches for large units (ask reception to open another gate for entry). All the 200 pitches have electricity (3/6A), 50 also have water and drainage, and there is an outside sink and cold water for every four. There is ample shade from mature trees and shrubs, which are constantly watered and cared for in summer. The 'gold' pitches and some wonderful tent pitches are along the seafront with great views. There is a path to a secluded and pleasant beach with sparkling waters, overlooked by a large patio area. The rocky surrounds are excellent for snorkelling and fishing, with ladder access to the water. The friendly management speak excellent English and will supply detailed touring plans. Activities and entertainment are organised in high season for adults and children.

You might like to know

There are many exciting events throughout the summer, including the 'corso fiorito' (floral exhibition) and the Spring Celebration.

- ☑ Multilingual children's club – pre-school
- ☑ Multilingual children's club – 5-10 year olds
- ☑ Multilingual children's club – 10-14 year olds
- ☑ Creative crafts
- ☑ Bicycle hire for children
- ☐ Facilities for children in wash blocks
- ☑ Children's pool
- ☑ Children's play area
- ☐ Crèche and/or babysitting
- ☑ Local information of interest for children

Facilities: Three clean and modern toilet blocks have British and Turkish style WCs and hot water throughout. Baby rooms. Facilities for disabled campers. Laundry facilities. Motorcaravan services. Bar sells essential supplies. Large restaurant. Pizzeria and takeaway (all year). Sea water swimming pools (small extra charge in high season) and heated whirlpool spa (June-Sept). Tennis. Excellent play area. Fishing. Satellite TV. Internet access. WiFi (free after 7 days hire). Bicycle hire. Gas delivered to pitch. Dogs are not accepted. Off site: Bus at gate. Supermarket 100 m. Shop 150 m. Riding and golf 2 km. 24 km. cycle route to the city.

Open: All year.

Directions: From SS1 (Ventimiglia - Imperia), site is on right just before San Remo. There is a sharp right turn if approaching from the west. From autostrada A10 take San Remo Ouest exit. Site is well signed. GPS: 43.80117, 7.74867

Charges guide

Per unit incl. 4 persons	€ 29,00 - € 60,00

ITALY – Ceriale

Camping Baciccia

Via Torino 19, I-17023 Ceriale (Ligúria)
t: **018 299 0743** e: **info@campingbaciccia.it**
alanrogers.com/IT64030 www.campingbaciccia.it

Accommodation: ☑ Pitch ☑ Mobile home/chalet ☐ Hotel/B&B ☐ Apartment

This friendly, family run site is a popular holiday destination. Baciccia was the nickname of the present owner's grandfather who grew fruit trees and tomatoes on the site. Tall eucalyptus trees shade the 106 flat pitches which encircle the central facilities block. The pitches are on flat ground and all have electricity. There is always a family member by the gate to greet you, and Vincenzina and Giovanni, along with their daughter and son, Laura and Mauro, work tirelessly to ensure that you enjoy your stay. The pool has a giant elephant slide and there is a vibrant play area for children. The informal restaurant serves delightful seasonal Italian dishes and overlooks a large swimming pool. There is a free shuttle to the site's private beach and the town has the usual seaside attractions. This site will suit campers looking for a family atmosphere with none of the brashness of large seaside sites. If you have forgotten anything by way of camping equipment just ask and the family will lend it to you.

Special offers
Special low-season offer: free shuttle bus to the private beach 1.5 km. away.

You might like to know
There is plenty to do off site – free beach (500 m), water park (500 m) and a fascinating aquarium (80 km).

☐ Multilingual children's club – pre-school
☐ Multilingual children's club – 5-10 year olds
☐ Multilingual children's club – 10-14 year olds
☑ Creative crafts
☐ Bicycle hire for children
☐ Facilities for children in wash blocks
☑ Children's pool
☑ Children's play area
☐ Crèche and/or babysitting
☑ Local information of interest for children

Facilities: Two clean and modern sanitary blocks near reception have British and Turkish style WCs and hot water throughout. Laundry. Motorcaravan services. Restaurant/bar. Shop. Pizzeria and takeaway. A swimming pool and paddling pool (1/4-31/10) and private beach. Tennis. Bowls. Excellent new play area. Bicycle hire. Wood-burning stove and barbecue. WiFi. Fishing. Diving. Entertainment for children and adults in high season. Excursions. Off site: Bus 200 m. Aquapark 500 m. Riding and golf 2 km. Ancient town of Albenga (2,000 years old) 3 km.

Open: 20 March - 3 November, 4 December - 10 January.

Directions: From the A10 between Imperia and Savona, take Albenga exit. Follow signs Ceriale, Savona and Aquapark Caravelle (which is 500 m. from site) and then site signs. Site is just south of Savona. GPS: 44.08165, 8.21763

Charges guide

Per unit incl. up to 3 persons (over 2 yrs)	€ 29,00 - € 49,00
extra person	€ 5,00 - € 10,00
dog	€ 2,00 - € 4,00

Camping Norcenni Girasole Club

Via Norcenni 7, I-50063 Figline Valdarno (Tuscany)
t: **055 915 141** e: **girasole@ecvacanze.it**
alanrogers.com/IT66120 www.ecvacanze.it

Accommodation: ☑ Pitch ☑ Mobile home/chalet ☐ Hotel/B&B ☐ Apartment

Norcenni Girasole Club is a brilliant, busy and well run resort style site in a picturesque, secluded situation with great views of Tuscan landscapes, 19 km. south of Florence. Owned by the dynamic Cardini-Vannucchi family, care has been taken in its development and the buildings and infrastructure are most attractive and in sympathy with the area. There are 160 roomy pitches for touring units, 136 with 6A electricity and 22 fully serviced including 16A electricity. Most are shaded by well tended trees. The ground is hard and stony. Although on a fairly steep hillside, pitches are on level terraces accessed from good, hard roads. In the large swimming pool complex there is a superb choice, with pools for children of all ages plus a free water flume. A small health complex offers saunas, jacuzzi, steam bath, fitness centre and massage. An extensive entertainment programme is available weekly with activities for children and adults, plus courses in Tuscan cooking, wine tasting and the Italian language.

You might like to know

The site is very close to Florence – this beautiful city is a must for visitors to Italy.

- ☑ Multilingual children's club – pre-school
- ☑ Multilingual children's club – 5-10 year olds
- ☑ Multilingual children's club – 10-14 year olds
- ☑ Creative crafts
- ☐ Bicycle hire for children
- ☐ Facilities for children in wash blocks
- ☑ Children's pool
- ☑ Children's play area
- ☐ Crèche and/or babysitting
- ☑ Local information of interest for children

Facilities: Sanitary facilities are very good with mixed British and Turkish style WCs. Hot water is available throughout. Family bathrooms for rent (book in advance). Facilities for disabled visitors. Laundry facilities. Supermarket and gift shops. Bar and three restaurants. Pizzeria. Gelateria. Swimming pools, one covered and heated (supervised; hats required). Pool bar, new pool with slide for small children (under 6 yrs). Fitness centre. Soundproofed disco. Two floodlit tennis courts. Riding. Minigolf. Bicycle hire. Internet access. ATM. Extensive entertainment programme. Excursions. Off site: Daily bus to Florence and shuttle buses to local railway station. Riding 3 km. Fishing 5 km. Golf 30 km.

Open: 16 April - 8 October.

Directions: From Florence take the Rome AI/E35 autostrada and take Incisa exit. Turn south on route 69 towards Arezzo. In Figline turn right for Greve and watch for Girasole signs - site is 4 km. up a twisting, climbing road. GPS: 43.61333, 11.44944

Charges guide

Per person	€ 7,00 - € 13,50
child (2-12 yrs)	free - € 7,50
pitch	€ 10,00 - € 29,50

ITALY – Martinsicuro

Camping Village Duca Amedeo

Lungomare Europa, 158, I-64014 Martinsicuro (Abruzzo)
t: **086 179 7376** e: **info@ducaamedeo.it**
alanrogers.com/IT67982 www.ducaamedeo.it

Accommodation: ☑ Pitch ☑ Mobile home/chalet ☐ Hotel/B&B ☐ Apartment

Duca Amadeo is in an attractive setting with direct access to a broad, sandy beach. The beach shelves very gradually and is therefore ideal for younger children. This site also enjoys the advantage of being set well back from the busy coastal railway line. There are 149 pitches here, of which 55 are available to tourers. These are of a reasonable size and most have electrical connections. There are also a number of chalets and wood-clad mobile homes for rent. Leisure facilities include an attractive swimming pool, with a wide sun terrace. The site is lively in high season with a varied programme of activities for all the family. The resort town of Martinsicuro is within walking distance and is a lovely place to explore. The town has a Roman history and the 16th-century Charles V Tower houses an interesting archaeological museum. Further afield, the Abruzzo national park merits exploration and fulfils an important conservation role in maintaining the habitat of the Italian wolf and Marsican brown bear.

You might like to know
The chalets and wood-clad mobile homes have air-conditioning and TV.

☐ Multilingual children's club – pre-school
☑ Multilingual children's club – 5-10 year olds
☑ Multilingual children's club – 10-14 year olds
☑ Creative crafts
☑ Bicycle hire for children
☑ Facilities for children in wash blocks
☑ Children's pool
☑ Children's play area
☐ Crèche and/or babysitting
☑ Local information of interest for children

Facilities: Swimming pool (with sun terrace and children's pool). Picnic area. Games room. Children's playground. Sports field. Beach volleyball. Activity and entertainment programme. Tourist information. Mobile homes and chalets for rent. Off site: Martinsicuro (shops, cafés and restaurants). Abruzzo national park.

Open: 23 April - 19 September.

Directions: The site is located on the seafront at Martinsicuro. Leave the A14 autostrada at the Martinsicuro exit, to the south of San Benedetto del Tronto. Follow signs to the town centre and then to the site. GPS: 42.88118, 13.9207

Charges guide

Per unit incl. 2 persons and electricity	€ 15,00 - € 42,00

ITALY – Baia Domizia

Baia Domizia Villaggio Camping

I-81030 Baia Domizia (Campania)
t: 082 393 0164 e: info@baiadomizia.it
alanrogers.com/IT68200 www.baiadomizia.it

Accommodation: ☑ Pitch ☑ Mobile home/chalet ☐ Hotel/B&B ☐ Apartment

This large, beautifully maintained seaside site is about 70 kilometres northwest of Naples, and is within a pine forest, cleverly left in its natural state. Although it does not feel like it, there are 750 touring pitches in clearings, either of grass and sand or on hardstanding, all with electricity. Finding a pitch may take time as there are so many good ones to choose from, but staff will help in season. Most pitches are well shaded, however there are some in the sun for cooler periods. The central complex is superb with well designed buildings providing for all needs (the site is some distance from the town). Restaurants, bars and a gelateria enjoy live entertainment and attractive water lily ponds surround the area. The entire site is attractive, with shrubs, flowers and huge green areas. A wide range of sports and other amenities are provided. Although the site is big, there is never very far to walk to the beach. This site is well above average and most suitable for families with children. Member of Leading Campings Group.

You might like to know

This is a very well equipped site, with an attractive shopping centre, a restaurant, a fruit and vegetable shop and four bars.

- ☑ Multilingual children's club – pre-school
- ☑ Multilingual children's club – 5-10 year olds
- ☑ Multilingual children's club – 10-14 year olds
- ☑ Creative crafts
- ☐ Bicycle hire for children
- ☐ Facilities for children in wash blocks
- ☑ Children's pool
- ☑ Children's play area
- ☐ Crèche and/or babysitting
- ☑ Local information of interest for children

Facilities: Seven new toilet blocks have hot water in washbasins (many cabins) and showers. Good access and facilities for disabled campers. Washing machines, spin dryers. Motorcaravan services. Gas supplies. Supermarket and general shop. Large bar. Restaurants, pizzeria and takeaway. Ice cream parlour. Swimming pool complex. Playground. Tennis. Windsurfing hire and school. Disco. Excursions. Dogs are not accepted. Off site: Bicycle hire 100 m. Fishing and riding 3 km.

Open: 5 May - 18 September.

Directions: The turn to Baia Domizia leads off the Formia - Naples road 23 km. from Formia. From Rome - Naples autostrada, take Cassino exit to Formia. Site is to the north of Baia Domizia and well signed. Site is off the coastal road that runs parallel to the SS7.
GPS: 41.207222, 13.791389

Charges guide

Per person	€ 5,50 - € 11,50
child (1-11 yrs)	€ 4,00 - € 8,50
pitch incl. electricity	€ 11,50 - € 23,00

Camping Lanterna

Lanterna 1, HR-52465 Porec (Istria)
t: 052 465 010   e: camping@valamar.com
alanrogers.com/CR6716   www.camping-adriatic.com

Accommodation: ☑ Pitch ☑ Mobile home/chalet ☐ Hotel/B&B ☐ Apartment

This is a well organised site and one of the largest in Croatia with high standards and an amazing selection of activities, and is part of the Camping on the Adriatic group. Set in 80 hectares with over 3 km. of beach, there are 2,851 pitches, of which 1,887 are for touring units. All have electricity (10A) and fresh water and 225 also have waste water drainage. Pitches are 80-120 sq.m. with some superb locations right on the sea, although these tend to be taken first so it is advisable to book ahead. Some of the better pitches are in a 'reserved booking' area. There are wonderful coastal views from some of the well shaded terraced pitches. Facilities at Lanterna are impressive with the whole operation running smoothly for the campers. The land is sloping in parts and terraced in others. There is a pool complex including a large pool for children, in addition to the pretty bay with its rocky beaches and buoyed safety areas. Many activities and quality entertainment for all are available both on and off site – you are spoilt for choice here, including a vast choice of places to eat.

You might like to know

There are no fewer than three supermarkets here catering for all your needs, as well as a fresh fish shop. The Istria Prestige mobile homes are available to rent, and are designed in an Istrian style.

- ☑ Multilingual children's club – pre-school
- ☑ Multilingual children's club – 5-10 year olds
- ☑ Multilingual children's club – 10-14 year olds
- ☐ Creative crafts
- ☐ Bicycle hire for children
- ☑ Facilities for children in wash blocks
- ☑ Children's pool
- ☑ Children's play area
- ☐ Crèche and/or babysitting
- ☑ Local information of interest for children

Facilities: The 16 sanitary blocks are clean and good quality. Children's facilities and baby care areas, some Turkish style WCs, hot showers. Some blocks have facilities for disabled visitors. Three supermarkets sell most everyday items. Fresh fish shop. Four restaurants, bars and snack bars and fast food outlets. Swimming pool and two paddling pools. Sandpit and play areas. Entertainment for all in high season. Tennis. Bicycle hire. Watersports. Boat hire. Minigolf. Riding. Internet café. Jetty and ramp for boats. WiFi (free). Pets are allowed in certain areas. Off site: Hourly bus service from the reception area. Fishing. Riding 500 m. Golf 2 km. Nearest large supermarket in Novigrad 9 km.

Open: 1 April - 10 October.

Directions: The turn to Lanterna is well signed off the Novigrad to Porec road about 8 km. south of Novigrad. Continue for about 2 km. turn off road towards the coast and the campsite is on right hand side. GPS: 45.29672, 13.59442

Charges guide

Per unit incl. 2 persons and electricity	€ 16,90 - € 31,00
with full services	€ 18,30 - € 32,60
extra person	€ 4,40 - € 7,90
child (4-10 yrs)	free - € 5,40

Naturist Camping Valalta

Cesta Valalta-Lim bb, HR-52210 Rovinj (Istria)
t: 052 804 800 e: valalta@valalta.hr
alanrogers.com/CR6731 www.valalta.hr

Accommodation: ☑ Pitch ☐ Mobile home/chalet ☐ Hotel/B&B ☐ Apartment

This is a most impressive site for up to 6,000 naturist campers, which has a pleasant, open feel. The passage through reception is efficient and this feeling is maintained around the well organised site. A friendly, family atmosphere is to be found here. Valalta is a family oriented campsite. All pitches are the same price with 16A electricity, although they vary in size and surroundings. The variations include shade, views, sand, grass, sea frontage, level ground, slopes and terracing. It is not possible to reserve a particular pitch and campers do move pitches at will. The impressive pool is in lagoon style with water features and cascades. Unusually for Croatia, the beach has soft sand (with some help from imported sand). All manner of sports are available and a marina forms part of the site. The high standard here and throughout the campsite has ensured that customers have returned regularly since its opening in 1968. We were impressed by this well ordered and smart naturist site.

You might like to know

Naturist tourers are sure to love this site with its fabulous marina, which caters for all types of sailing requirements.

- ☑ Multilingual children's club – pre-school
- ☑ Multilingual children's club – 5-10 year olds
- ☑ Multilingual children's club – 10-14 year olds
- ☐ Creative crafts
- ☐ Bicycle hire for children
- ☑ Facilities for children in wash blocks
- ☑ Children's pool
- ☑ Children's play area
- ☐ Crèche and/or babysitting
- ☑ Local information of interest for children

Facilities: Twenty high quality new or refurbished sanitary blocks of which four are smaller units of plastic 'pod' construction. Hot showers (coin operated). Facilities for disabled campers. Washing machines and dryers. Supermarket. Four restaurants (one specialising in seafood). Pizzeria. Two bars. Large lagoon style pool complex. Beauty salon. Fitness club. Massage. Minigolf. Tennis. Sailing. Play area. Bicycle hire. Beach volleyball. Marina with full services. Internet. Entertainment all season. Kindergarten. Dogs are not accepted. Off site: Riding 7 km.

Open: 25 April - 26 September.

Directions: Site is on the coast 8 km. north of Rovinj. If approaching from the north turn inland (follow signs to Rovinj) to drive around the Limski Kanal. Then follow signs towards Valalta 2 km. east of Rovinj. Site is at the end of the road and is well signed. GPS: 45.12235, 13.632083

Charges guide

Per unit incl. 2 persons and electricity	€ 26,80 - € 44,80
extra person	€ 8,80 - € 16,30
child (4-14 yrs)	€ 2,50 - € 5,50

CROATIA – Mali Losinj

Camp Cikat

Cikat 13, HR-51550 Mali Losinj (Kvarner)
t: **051 232125** e: **info@camp-cikat.com**
alanrogers.com/CR6754 www.camps-cres-losinj.com/cikat

Accommodation: ☑ Pitch ☑ Mobile home/chalet ☐ Hotel/B&B ☐ Apartment

This site is the largest on the island of Losinj and has a range of pitches on offer, most with electricity. Cikat has direct access to the sea and a number of premium pitches are available at the water's edge (supplement applies). The beach is mostly rocky, with paved sunbathing areas. It is backed by a pine forest and has two small coves, ideal for younger children. The campsite restaurant specialises in local cuisine, notably Cres lamb and locally-caught fish and seafood. The site supermarket is open throughout the season (with a fresh fruit and vegetable section in peak season). Losinj is a great base for an active holiday. Snorkelling and diving are both understandably popular and lessons are available. Boat trips are organised to neighbouring islands. Settlement on the island dates back to prehistoric times and there are traces of hill forts close to the modern port of Mali Losinj. More recently, remains of Roman history can found in a number of beautiful preserved churches.

You might like to know

The Pepé Family Fun Park is a great play area with 500 sq.m. of space – 200 sq.m. indoors and a 300 sq.m. outdoor go-kart track. To the best of our knowledge it is the first children's play area to be built as an on-site facility in Croatia, and perhaps even in Europe.

- ☑ Multi-lingual children's club – pre-school
- ☑ Multi-lingual children's club – 5-10 year olds
- ☑ Multi-lingual children's club – 10-14 year olds
- ☑ Creative crafts
- ☑ Bicycle hire for children
- ☑ Facilities for children in wash blocks
- ☐ Children's pool
- ☑ Children's play area
- ☑ Crèche and/or babysitting
- ☑ Local information of interest for children

Facilities: Shop. Bar, snack bar and restaurant. Fishing. Massage. Play area. Entertainment and activity programme. Mobile homes and chalets to rent. Direct sea access. Pebble beach. Off site; Riding. Cycle and walking tracks. Boat trips to neighbouring islands.

Open: 5 April - 20 October.

Directions: Upon arrival on the island of Cres, head south on road 100 crossing onto the island of Losinj and continue to Mali Losinj. From here follow signs to the site. GPS: 44.53596, 14.4509

Charges guide

Per unit incl. 2 persons	
and electricity	€ 15,00 - € 23,00
dog	€ 2,20 - € 3,00

Balatontourist Camping Napfény

Halász u. 5, H-8253 Révfülöp (Veszprem County)
t: 87 563 031   e: napfeny@balatontourist.hu
alanrogers.com/HU5370   www.balatontourist.hu

Accommodation: ☑ Pitch ☑ Mobile home/chalet ☐ Hotel/B&B ☐ Apartment

Camping Napfény, an exceptionally good site, is designed for families with children of all ages looking for an active holiday, and has a 200 m. frontage on Lake Balaton. The site's 370 pitches vary in size (60-110 sq.m) and almost all have shade – very welcome during the hot Hungarian summers – and 6-10A electricity. As with most of the sites on Lake Balaton, a train line runs just outside the site boundary. There are steps to get into the lake, and canoes, boats and pedalos are for hire. An extensive entertainment programme is designed for all ages and there are several bars and restaurants of various styles. There are souvenir shops and a supermarket. In fact, you need not leave the site at all during your holiday, although there are several excursions on offer, including to Budapest or to one of the many Hungarian spas, a trip over Lake Balaton or a traditional wine tour.

You might like to know

Camping Napfény is in a great location with direct access to Lake Balaton, where children can play safely on the small, sandy beach.

☐ Multilingual children's club – pre-school
☑ Multilingual children's club – 5-10 year olds
☑ Multilingual children's club – 10-14 year olds
☑ Creative crafts
☑ Bicycle hire for children
☑ Facilities for children in wash blocks
☑ Children's pool
☑ Children's play area
☐ Crèche and/or babysitting
☑ Local information of interest for children

Facilities: The three excellent sanitary blocks have toilets, washbasins (open style and in cabins) with hot and cold water, spacious showers (both preset and controllable), child size toilets and basins, and two bathrooms (hourly charge). Heated baby room. Facilities for disabled campers. Launderette. Motorcaravan services. Supermarket. Several bars, restaurants and souvenir shop. Children's pool. Sports field. Minigolf. Fishing. Bicycle hire. Canoe, rowing boats and pedalo hire. Extensive entertainment programme for all ages. Internet access (charged). Off site: Tennis 300 m. Riding 3 km.

Open: 30 April - 30 September.

Directions: Follow road 71 from Veszprém southeast to Keszthely. Site is in Révfülöp. GPS: 46.829469, 17.640164

Charges guide

Per unit incl. 2 persons and electricity	HUF 3400 - 7150
extra person	HUF 800 - 1200
child (2-14 yrs)	HUF 550 - 900
dog	HUF 550 - 900

Ferienparadies Natterer See

Natterer See 1, A-6161 Natters (Tirol)
t: **051 254 6732** e: **info@natterersee.com**
alanrogers.com/AU0060 www.natterersee.com

Accommodation: ☑Pitch ☐ Mobile home/chalet ☑Hotel/B&B ☑ Apartment

In a quiet location arranged around two lakes and set amid beautiful alpine scenery, this site founded in 1930 is renowned as one of Austria's top sites. Over the last few years a lot of improvement work has been carried out and pride of place on site is a new, innovative, award-winning multifunctional building. This contains all of the sanitary facilities expected of a top site including a special children's section, private bathrooms to rent, a dog bath, plus reception, shop, café/bar/bistro and cinema, and on the upper floor a panorama lounge as well as a large collection of model cars. Almost all of the 235 pitches are for touring units. They are terraced, set on gravel/grass, all have electricity and most offer a splendid view of the mountains. The site's lakeside restaurant with bar and large terrace has a good menu and is the ideal place to spend the evening. With a bus every hour and the city centre only 19 minutes away this is also a good site from which to visit the city.

You might like to know
The new wash block is second to none, with amazing 'thunder and lightning' showers, great fun for children!

☐ Multilingual children's club – pre-school
☑ Multilingual children's club – 5-10 year olds
☑ Multilingual children's club – 10-14 year olds
☑ Creative crafts
☑ Bicycle hire for children
☑ Facilities for children in wash blocks
☑ Children's pool
☑ Children's play area
☑ Crèche and/or babysitting
☑ Local information of interest for children

Facilities: The large sanitary blocks have underfloor heating, some washbasins in cabins, plus excellent facilities for babies, children and disabled visitors. Laundry facilities. Motorcaravan services. Bar. Restaurant and takeaway (20/3-3/10). Pizzeria. Good shop. Playgrounds. Children's activity programme. Child minding (day nursery) in high season. Sports field. Archery. Youth room with games, pool and billiards. TV room with Sky. Internet point and WiFi. Open air cinema. Mountain bike hire. Aquapark (1/5-30/9). Surf bikes and pedalos. Canoes and mini sailboats for rent. Entertainment programme (mid May-mid Oct). Dogs are not accepted in high season (July/Aug). Off site: Tennis and minigolf nearby. Riding 6 km. Golf 12 km.

Open: All year excl. 31 October - 14 December.

Directions: From Inntal autobahn (A12) take Brenner autobahn (A13) as far as Innsbruck-sud/Natters exit (no. 3). Turn left by petrol station onto the B182 to Natters. At roundabout take first exit and immediately right again and follow signs to site 4 km. GPS: 47.23755, 11.34201

Charges guide

Per unit incl. 2 persons and electricity	€ 25,20 - € 42,00
extra person	€ 5,90 - € 8,20
child (under 13 yrs)	€ 4,60 - € 6,00

Camping Seeblick Toni

Reintalersee, Moosen 46, A-6233 Kramsach (Tirol)
t: 053 376 3544 e: info@camping-seeblick.at
alanrogers.com/AU0100 www.camping-seeblick.at

Accommodation: ☑Pitch ☑Mobile home/chalet ☐ Hotel/B&B ☐ Apartment

Austria has some of the finest sites in Europe and Seeblick Toni is one of them.
In a quiet, rural situation on the edge of the small Reintalersee lake, it is well worth
considering for holidays in the Tirol with many excursions possible. The surrounding
mountains give scenic views and the campsite has a neat and tidy appearance. The
243 level pitches (215 for touring units) are in regular rows off hard access roads and
are a good size with grass and hardstanding. All pitches have electricity (10A), 150 are
fully serviced including cable TV and phone connections. The large, well appointed
restaurant has a roof-top terrace where one can enjoy a meal, drink or snack and admire
the lovely scenery. A path leads to the lake for swimming, boating and a sunbathing
meadow. With a good solarium, sauna, whirlpool and fitness centre, this site provides
for an excellent summer holiday and, with ski areas near, an excellent winter holiday
also. This is a family run site with good English spoken and there is a friendly welcome.

You might like to know
The Topi Club is great fun, and one reason
why many families return here year after year.

☑ Multilingual children's club – pre-school
☑ Multilingual children's club – 5-10 year olds
☑ Multilingual children's club – 10-14 year olds
☐ Creative crafts
☐ Bicycle hire for children
☑ Facilities for children in wash blocks
☐ Children's pool
☑ Children's play area
☐ Crèche and/or babysitting
☑ Local information of interest
for children

Facilities: Two outstanding sanitary blocks
(heated in cool weather). One includes en-suite
toilet/basin/shower rooms, the other also has
individual bathrooms to rent. Facilities for
disabled visitors. New facilities for children. Baby
room. Laundry facilities. Drying rooms. Freezer.
Motorcaravan services. Restaurant. Bar. Snack
kiosk. Shop. Fitness centre. Playground. New
indoor play area. 'Topi' club, kindergarten and
organised activities for children in high season.
Youth room. Fishing. Bicycle hire. Riding. Internet.
Off site: Kramsach 3 km.

Open: All year.

Directions: Take exit 32 for Kramsach from the
A12 autobahn and turn right at roundabout, then
immediately left following signs 'Zu den Seen' in
village. After 3 km. turn right at site sign. Note:
there are two sites side by side at the lake;
Seeblick Toni is the second one reached. Do not
rely on sat nav. GPS: 47.46104, 11.90676

Charges guide

Per unit incl. 2 persons	
and electricity	€ 29,50 - € 40,50
extra person	€ 7,50 - € 10,00
child (under 14 yrs)	€ 5,00 - € 6,00
dog	€ 4,20 - € 5,50

AUSTRIA – Bruck

Sportcamp Woferlgut

Kroessenbach 40, A-5671 Bruck (Salzburg)
t: 065 457 3030 e: info@sportcamp.at
alanrogers.com/AU0180 www.sportcamp.at

Accommodation: ☑ Pitch ☐ Mobile home/chalet ☑ Hotel/B&B ☑ Apartment

The village of Bruck lies at the junction of the B311 and the Grossglocknerstrasse in the Hohe Tauern National Park. Sportcamp Woferlgut, a family run site, is one of the best in Austria. Surrounded by mountains, the site is quite flat with pleasant views. The 350 level, grass pitches are marked out by shrubs (300 for touring units) and each has electricity (16A), water, drainage, cable TV socket and gas point. A high grass bank separates the site and the road. The site's own lake, used for swimming and fishing, is surrounded by a landscaped sunbathing area. The fitness centre has a fully equipped gym, whilst another building contains a sauna and cold dip, Turkish bath, solarium (all free), massage on payment and a bar. In summer there is a free activity programme, evenings with live music, club for children, weekly barbecues and guided cycle and mountain tours. In winter a cross country skiing trail and toboggan run lead from the site and a free bus service is provided to nearby skiing facilities. Good English is spoken.

You might like to know
In June 2011, Woferlgut introduced a new Family Experience Adventure Golf – great fun for all the family!

- ☑ Multilingual children's club – pre-school
- ☑ Multilingual children's club – 5-10 year olds
- ☑ Multilingual children's club – 10-14 year olds
- ☑ Creative crafts
- ☐ Bicycle hire for children
- ☐ Facilities for children in wash blocks
- ☑ Children's pool
- ☑ Children's play area
- ☐ Crèche and/or babysitting
- ☑ Local information of interest for children

Facilities: Three modern sanitary blocks have excellent facilities, including private cabins, underfloor heating and music. Washing machines and dryers. Facilities for disabled visitors. Family bathrooms for hire. Motorcaravan services. Well stocked shop. Bar, restaurant and takeaway. Small, heated outdoor pool and children's pool (1/5-30/9). Fitness centre. Two playgrounds, indoor play room and children's cinema. Tennis. Bicycle hire. Fishing. Watersports and lake swimming. Collection of small animals with pony-rides for young children. WiFi. Off site: Skiing 2.5 km. Golf 3 km. Boat launching and sailing 3.5 km. Hiking and skiing (all year) nearby.

Open: All year.

Directions: Site is southwest of Bruck. From road B311, Bruck by-pass, take southern exit (Grossglockner) and site is signed from the junction of B311 and B107 roads (small signs). GPS: 47.2838, 12.81694

Charges guide

Per unit incl. 2 persons and electricity (plus meter)	€ 21,90 - € 34,50
extra person	€ 5,10 - € 8,20
child (2-10 yrs)	€ 4,10 - € 6,10
dog	€ 3,10 - € 4,30

AUSTRIA – Döbriach

Komfort-Campingpark Burgstaller

Seefeldstrasse 16, A-9873 Döbriach (Carinthia)
t: 042 467 774 e: info@burgstaller.co.at
alanrogers.com/AU0480 www.komfortcamping.at

Accommodation: ☑ Pitch ☐ Mobile home/chalet ☐ Hotel/B&B ☐ Apartment

This is one of Austria's top sites in a beautiful location and with all the amenities you could want. You can always tell a true family run site by the attention to detail and this site oozes perfection. This is an excellent family site with a very friendly atmosphere, particularly in the restaurant in the evenings. Good English is spoken. The 600 pitches (560 for tourists) are on flat, well drained grass, backing onto hedges on either side of the access roads. All fully serviced (including WiFi), they vary in size (45-120 sq.m) and there are special pitches for motorcaravans. One pitch actually rotates and follows the sun during the course of the day! The latest sanitary block warrants an architectural award; all toilets have a TV and a pirate ship on the first floor of the children's area sounds its guns every hour. The site entrance is directly opposite the park leading to the bathing lido, to which campers have free access. There is also a heated swimming pool. Much activity is organised here, including games and competitions for children.

You might like to know

There's some really imaginative entertainment for children, such as searching for precious stones!

- ☑ Multilingual children's club – pre-school
- ☑ Multilingual children's club – 5-10 year olds
- ☑ Multilingual children's club – 10-14 year olds
- ☑ Creative crafts
- ☐ Bicycle hire for children
- ☑ Facilities for children in wash blocks
- ☐ Children's pool
- ☑ Children's play area
- ☐ Crèche and/or babysitting
- ☑ Local information of interest for children

Facilities: Three exceptionally good quality toilet blocks include washbasins in cabins, facilities for children and disabled visitors, dishwashers and underfloor heating. Seven private rooms for rent (3 with jacuzzi baths). Motorcaravan services. Bar. Good restaurant with terrace (May-Oct). Shop (May-Sept). Bowling alley. Disco (July/Aug). TV room. Sauna and solarium. Two play areas (one for under 6s, the other for 6-12 yrs). Bathing and boating on lake. Special entrance rate for lake attractions. Fishing. Bicycle hire. Riding. Comprehensive entertainment programmes. Covered stage and outdoor arena provide for church services and folk and modern music concerts. Off site: Mountain walks, climbing and farm visits all in local area.

Open: 4 April - 5 November.

Directions: Leave A10 at exit 139 (Spittal, Millstätter) then proceed alongside northern shore of lake through Millstätter towards Döbriach. Just before Döbriach turn right and after 1 km. site is on left. GPS: 46.77151, 13.64918

Charges guide

Per unit incl. 2 persons and electricity	€ 19,10 - € 34,00
extra person	€ 7,00 - € 10,00
child (4-14 yrs)	€ 5,00 - € 8,00

Camping Campofelice

Via alle Brere 7, CH-6598 Tenero (Ticino)
t: **091 745 1417** e: **camping@campofelice.ch**
alanrogers.com/CH9890 www.campofelice.ch

Accommodation: ☑Pitch ☐ Mobile home/chalet ☐ Hotel/B&B ☐ Apartment

The largest site in Switzerland, it is bordered on the front by Lake Maggiore and on one side by the Verzasca estuary, where the site has its own marina. Campofelice is divided into rows, with 860 generously sized, individual pitches on flat grass on either side of hard access roads. Mostly well shaded, all pitches have electricity connections (10-13A) and 409 also have water, drainage and TV connections. Pitches near the lake cost more (these are not available for motorcaravans until September) and a special area is reserved for small tents. The sheer quality of this superb site justifies the higher than average prices. Sporting facilities are good and there are cycle paths in the area, including into Locarno. The beach by the lake is sandy, long and wider than the usual lakeside ones. It shelves gently so that bathing is safe for children. Within a demarcated area are floating trampolines and rafts, and a specially marked section for toddlers.

You might like to know

There's a tree-top adventure park here, where your children can climb in complete safety, supervised by qualified instructors.

- ☑ Multilingual children's club – pre-school
- ☑ Multilingual children's club – 5-10 year olds
- ☑ Multilingual children's club – 10-14 year olds
- ☑ Creative crafts
- ☑ Bicycle hire for children
- ☐ Facilities for children in wash blocks
- ☐ Children's pool
- ☑ Children's play area
- ☐ Crèche and/or babysitting
- ☑ Local information of interest for children

Facilities: The six toilet blocks (three heated) are of exemplary quality. Washing machines and dryers. Motorcaravan services. Gas supplies. Supermarket, restaurant, bar and takeaway (all season). Snack kiosk at beach. Lifeguards on duty. Tennis. Minigolf. Bicycle hire. Canoe and pedalo hire. Boat launching. Playgrounds. Doctor calls. Dogs are not accepted. New chalet for disabled visitors. Camping accessories shop. Car hire. Car wash. WiFi (charged). Off site: Fishing 500 m. Water skiing and windsurfing 1 km. Riding 5 km. Golf 8 km. Boatyard with maintenance facilities.

Open: 22 March - 31 October.

Directions: On the Bellinzona - Locarno road 13, exit Tenero. Site is signed at roundabout. Coming from the south, enter Tenero and follow signs to site. GPS: 46.168611, 8.855556

Charges guide

Per unit incl. 2 persons and electricity	€ 38,00 - € 82,00
extra person	€ 8,00 - € 11,00

FRANCE – Vallon-Pont-d'Arc

Camping la Roubine

Route de Ruoms, F-07150 Vallon-Pont-d'Arc (Ardèche)
t: **04 75 88 04 56** e: **roubine.ardeche@wanadoo.fr**
alanrogers.com/FR07310 www.camping-roubine.com

Accommodation: ☑ Pitch ☑ Mobile home/chalet ☐ Hotel/B&B ☐ Apartment

This site on the bank of the Ardèche has been in the same family ownership for some 30 years. During this time there has been constant upgrading and it must now be considered one of the best sites in the area. There are 114 touring pitches, all with electricity (10A) and quite spacious. Well tended grass, trimmed hedging, and mature trees and smart tarmac roads create a calm and well kept atmosphere. The proprietors, M. Moulin and Mme. Van Eck like to welcome their guests and are available to help during the day – they are rightly proud of their well run campsite. Much attention is given to cleanliness – the toilet blocks are cleaned three times a day. A variety of sporting facilities are available on the site. The pool complex is heated when necessary throughout the season. The campsite also caters for their young visitors with children's club in high season complete with an adventure playground and even an amphitheatre. There is an Internet room for visitors.

You might like to know
On this bicycle-friendly site you will find a magical water playground, and in high season free magic and circus workshops, a children's club and supervised fishing trips for youngsters.

- ☐ Multilingual children's club – pre-school
- ☑ Multilingual children's club – 5-10 year olds
- ☑ Multilingual children's club – 10-14 year olds
- ☑ Creative crafts
- ☐ Bicycle hire for children
- ☑ Facilities for children in wash blocks
- ☑ Children's pool
- ☑ Children's play area
- ☐ Crèche and/or babysitting
- ☑ Local information of interest for children

Facilities: Several small sanitary blocks include washbasins in cubicles. The main toilet block has showers, washbasins in vanity units, a baby bathroom and facilities for disabled visitors. Laundry. Swimming pools, paddling pool and separate children's pool. Tennis. Boules. Fishing. Barbecues only permitted on communal sites. River beach. Off site: Footpath to town 700 m. Supermarket in town. Bicycle hire and riding 1 km.

Open: 26 April - 18 September.

Directions: From Vallon take the D579 towards Ruoms. Site is well signed on left 400 m. from town. From west (Ruoms) site signed on right near Vallon town sign. If missed proceed to roundabout at entrance to Vallon, go around and return some 400 m. (as above). GPS: 44.40547, 4.37916

Charges guide

Per unit incl. 2 persons and electricity	€ 22,50 - € 45,00
extra person	€ 3,40 - € 9,20
child (0-13 yrs)	€ 1,50 - € 8,00
dog	free - € 4,00

FRANCE – Salles-Curan

Kawan Village les Genêts

Lac de Pareloup, F-12410 Salles-Curan (Aveyron)
t: 05 65 46 35 34 e: contact@camping-les-genets.fr
alanrogers.com/FR12080 www.camping-les-genets.fr

Accommodation: ☑Pitch ☑Mobile home/chalet ☐ Hotel/B&B ☐ Apartment

The 163 pitches include 80 grassy, mostly individual pitches for touring units. These are in two areas, one on each side of the entrance lane, and are divided by hedges, shrubs and trees. Most have 6A electricity and many also have water and waste water drainage. The site slopes gently down to the beach and lake with facilities for all watersports including water skiing. A full animation and activities programme is organised in high season, and there is much to see and do in this very attractive corner of Aveyron. This family run site is on the shores of Lac de Pareloup and offers both family holiday and watersports facilities. The site is used by tour operators (25 pitches). The site is not suitable for American style motorhomes.

You might like to know
The beautiful Aveyron region offers numerous opportunities for excursions, be it a romantic getaway for two, or a fun day out for the whole family.

☑ Multilingual children's club – pre-school
☑ Multilingual children's club – 5-10 year olds
☑ Multilingual children's club – 10-14 year olds
☑ Creative crafts
☐ Bicycle hire for children
☑ Facilities for children in wash blocks
☑ Children's pool
☑ Children's play area
☐ Crèche and/or babysitting
☑ Local information of interest for children

Facilities: Two sanitary units, one refurbished, with suite for disabled guests. Baby room. Laundry. Well stocked shop (from 1/6). Bar, restaurant, snacks (14/6-5/9). Swimming pool, spa pool (from 1/6; unsupervised). Playground. Minigolf. Boules. Bicycle hire. Pedaloes, windsurfers, kayaks. Fishing licences available. WiFi in bar.

Open: 21 May - 11 September.

Directions: From Salles-Curan take D577 for about 4 km. and turn right into a narrow lane immediately after a sharp right hand bend. Site is signed at junction. GPS: 44.18933, 2.76693

Charges guide

Per unit incl. 2 persons and electricity	€ 18,00 - € 40,00
extra person	€ 4,00 - € 8,00
child (2-7 yrs)	free - € 7,00
pet	€ 3,00 - € 4,00

FRANCE – Saint Just-Luzac

Castel Camping Séquoia Parc

La Josephtrie, F-17320 Saint Just-Luzac (Charente-Maritime)
t: 05 46 85 55 55 e: info@sequoiaparc.com
alanrogers.com/FR17140 www.sequoiaparc.com

Accommodation: ☑Pitch ☑Mobile home/chalet ☐ Hotel/B&B ☐ Apartment

This is definitely a site not to be missed. Approached by an avenue of flowers, shrubs and trees, Séquoia Parc is a Castel site set in the grounds of La Josephtrie, a striking château with beautifully restored outbuildings and courtyard area with a bar and restaurant. Most of the 426 pitches are 140 sq.m. with 6/10A electricity connections and separated by mature shrubs providing plenty of privacy. The site has 300 mobile homes and chalets. This is a popular site with a children's club and entertainment throughout the season and reservation is necessary in high season. The site itself is designed to a high specification with reception in a large, light and airy room retaining its original beams and leading to the courtyard area where you find the bar and restaurant. The pool complex with water slides, large paddling pool and sunbathing area is impressive. A terraced area adjacent to the snack bar allows you to sit in a very pleasant garden setting with sunshades, to eat your meal. A member of Leading Campings Group.

You might like to know
Séquoia Parc was voted Best Family Campsite by ANWB in the Netherlands in 2011. The Ibou children's club is open for the entire season.

- ☐ Multilingual children's club – pre-school
- ☑ Multilingual children's club – 5-10 year olds
- ☑ Multilingual children's club – 10-14 year olds
- ☑ Creative crafts
- ☑ Bicycle hire for children
- ☑ Facilities for children in wash blocks
- ☑ Children's pool
- ☑ Children's play area
- ☐ Crèche and/or babysitting
- ☑ Local information of interest for children

Facilities: Three spotlessly clean luxurious toilet blocks, include facilities for children and disabled visitors. Dishwashing sinks. Large laundry. Motorcaravan service point. Gas supplies. Large supermarket. Boutique. Restaurant/bar and takeaway. Swimming pool complex with water slides and large paddling pool. Massage parlour (July/Aug). Multisports pitch. Tennis. Games and TV rooms. Bicycle hire. Updated play areas. Pony trekking. Organised entertainment/excursions all season. Children's farm. WiFi (charged). Off site: Supermarket and bank 5 km. Fishing 5 km. Golf 15 km. Flying trips. Ile d'Oléron.

Open: 14 May - 4 September (with all services).

Directions: Site is 5 km. southeast of Marennes. From Rochefort take D733 south for 12 km. Turn west on D123 to Ile d'Oléron. After 12 km. turn southeast on D728 (Saintes). Site signed, in 1 km. on left. From A10 at Saintes take D728 and leave this road by turning right shortly after St Just. Site signed. GPS: 45.81095, -1.06109

Charges guide

Per unit incl. 2 persons and electricity	€ 20,00 - € 47,00
extra person	€ 7,00 - € 9,00
child (3-12 yrs)	€ 3,00 - € 5,00
dog	€ 5,00

FRANCE – Saint Pardoux-la-Riviere

Kawan Village Château le Verdoyer

Champs Romain, F-24470 Saint Pardoux-la-Riviere (Dordogne)
t: 05 53 56 94 64   e: chateau@verdoyer.fr
alanrogers.com/FR24010   www.verdoyer.fr

Accommodation: ☑Pitch ☑Mobile home/chalet ☑Hotel/B&B ☐ Apartment

This 26-hectare estate has three lakes, two for fishing and one with a sandy beach and safe swimming area. There are 135 good sized touring pitches, level, terraced and hedged. With a choice of wooded area or open field, all have electricity (5/10A) and most share a water supply between four pitches. There is a swimming pool complex and high season activities are organised for children (5-13 yrs) but there is no disco. This site is well adapted for those with disabilities, with two fully adapted chalets, wheelchair access to all facilities and even a lift into the pool. Château le Verdoyer has been developed in the park of a restored château and is owned by a Dutch family. We particularly like this site for its beautiful buildings and lovely surroundings. It is situated in the lesser known area of the Dordogne sometimes referred to as the Périgord Vert, with its green forests and small lakes. The courtyard area between reception and the bar is home to evening activities, and provides a pleasant place to enjoy a drink and relax.

Special offers
Children under 5 go free all season!

You might like to know
Kawan Village Chateau le Verdoyer is in the heart of the Limousin National Park, this is a beautiful area for the whole family to enjoy.

- ☐ Multilingual children's club – pre-school
- ☑ Multilingual children's club – 5-10 year olds
- ☐ Multilingual children's club – 10-14 year olds
- ☑ Creative crafts
- ☑ Bicycle hire for children
- ☑ Facilities for children in wash blocks
- ☑ Children's pool
- ☑ Children's play area
- ☐ Crèche and/or babysitting
- ☑ Local information of interest for children

Facilities: Well appointed toilet blocks include facilities for disabled visitors and baby baths. Serviced launderette. Motorcaravan services. Fridge rental. Shop with gas (from 1/5). Bar, snacks, takeaway and restaurant (from 1/5). Bistro (July/Aug). Two pools, the smaller covered in low season, slide, paddling pool. Play areas. Tennis. Minigolf. Bicycle hire. Fishing. Small library. WiFi (charged). Computer in reception for Internet access. International newspapers daily. Off site: Riding 5 km. Golf 33 km. 'Circuit des Orchidées' (22 species of orchid). Vélo-rail at Bussière Galant. Market (Thursday and Sunday) at Saint Pardoux 12 km.

Open: 28 April - 30 September.

Directions: Site is 2 km. from the Limoges (N21) - Chalus (D6bis-D85) - Nontron road, 20 km. south of Chalus and is well signed from main road. Site on D96 about 4 km. north of village of Champs Romain. GPS: 45.55035, 0.7947

Charges guide

Per unit incl. 2 persons and electricity	€ 21,00 - € 38,50
extra person	€ 5,00 - € 6,50
child (6-11 yrs)	€ 4,00 - € 5,00
dog	€ 3,00 - € 4,00

Camping le Pech Charmant

F-24620 Les Eyzies-de-Tayac (Dordogne)
t: **05 53 35 97 08** e: **info@lepech.com**
alanrogers.com/FR24370 www.lepech.com

Accommodation: ☑Pitch ☑Mobile home/chalet ☐ Hotel/B&B ☐ Apartment

This site with a charming name is set on the top of a hill in the heart of the Périgord Noir, yet just 2 km. from Les Eyzies. The site is on two levels and the lower, quieter level has a spacious feeling with touring caravans and tents being positioned around its perimeter, leaving the centre clear. There are 80 level pitches, of which 10 are used for mobile homes and 2 new chalets. The pitches have dappled shade and 10A electricity. Donkey renting is popular with donkeys being used to help out with walks lasting from half a day to 3 days and more. The emphasis here is on the family and the activities are numerous. An adventure camp for 13-17 year olds is popular and this runs from Monday to Friday. A children's farm has a number of animals and a club is organised for children daily in high season. There is a snack bar with themed menus. Many interesting historical sites to visit in this area include caves, châteaux and museums.

You might like to know

The site is in the heart of the Dordogne with its castles, prehistoric ruins and breathtaking scenery. You can even rent a donkey – the children will love taking it for a walk!

- ☐ Multilingual children's club – pre-school
- ☑ Multilingual children's club – 5-10 year olds
- ☑ Multilingual children's club – 10-14 year olds
- ☑ Creative crafts
- ☐ Bicycle hire for children
- ☑ Facilities for children in wash blocks
- ☑ Children's pool
- ☑ Children's play area
- ☐ Crèche and/or babysitting
- ☑ Local information of interest for children

Facilities: Sanitary block with facilities for disabled visitors. Bar. Restaurant/snack bar. Takeaway. TV, internet access and WiFi in the bar. Swimming and paddling pools. Boules. Play area. Private access to the river. Fishing. Sports field. Only gas barbecues are permitted. American type motorhomes are not accepted. Off site: Bicycle hire 2 km. Riding 3 km. Golf 13 km.

Open: 15 April - 1 October.

Directions: From Les Eyzies head south on the D706 towards Le Bugue. Turn left immediately after the Renault garage and follow road for about 2 km. Site is signed along this road. GPS: 44.92404, 1.02982

Charges guide

Per unit incl. 2 persons and electricity	€ 12,00 - € 20,00
extra person	€ 3,00 - € 5,50
child (3-8 yrs)	€ 2,50 - € 4,15
dog	€ 1,50

FRANCE – Locunolé

Castel Camping le Ty-Nadan

Route d'Arzano, F-29310 Locunolé (Finistère)
t: 02 98 71 75 47   e: infos@camping-ty-nadan.fr
alanrogers.com/FR29010 www.camping-ty-nadan.fr

Accommodation: ☑Pitch ☑Mobile home/chalet   ☐ Hotel/B&B ☐ Apartment

Camping le Ty-Nadan is a well organised site set amongst wooded countryside along the bank of the River Elle. There are 183 grassy pitches for touring units, many with shade and 99 fully serviced. The pool complex with slides and paddling pool is very popular as are the large indoor pool complex and indoor games area with a climbing wall. There is also an adventure play park and a Minikids park for 5-8 year olds, not to mention tennis courts, table tennis, pool tables, archery and trampolines. This is a wonderful site for families with children. Several tour operators use the site.
An exciting and varied programme of activities is offered throughout the season – canoeing and sea kayaking expeditions, rock climbing, mountain biking, aquagym, paintball, horse riding or walking – all supervised by qualified staff. A full programme of entertainment for all ages is provided in high season including concerts, Breton evenings with pig roasts, dancing, etc. (be warned, you will be actively encouraged to join in!)

You might like to know
It's well worth making the trip to Devil's Rocks, either on foot, or by canoe if you're feeling brave!

☑ Multilingual children's club – pre-school
☑ Multilingual children's club – 5-10 year olds
☑ Multilingual children's club – 10-14 year olds
☑ Creative crafts
☑ Bicycle hire for children
☑ Facilities for children in wash blocks
☑ Children's pool
☐ Children's play area
☑ Crèche and/or babysitting
☑ Local information of interest for children

Facilities: Two older, split-level toilet blocks are of fair quality and include washbasins in cabins and baby rooms. A newer block provides easier access for disabled campers. Washing machines and dryers. Restaurant, takeaway, bar and well stocked shop. Heated outdoor pool (17x8 m). Indoor pool. Small river beach (unfenced). Indoor badminton and rock climbing facility. Activity and entertainment programmes (all season). Horse riding centre. Bicycle hire. Boat hire. Canoe trips. Fishing. Internet access and WiFi (charged). Off site: Beaches 20 minutes by car. Golf 12 km.

Open: 27 March - 2 September.

Directions: Make for Arzano which is northeast of Quimperlé on the Pontivy road and turn off D22 just west of village at site sign. Site is about 3 km. GPS: 47.90468, -3.47477

Charges guide

Per unit incl. 2 persons and electricity	€ 20,10 - € 46,00
extra person	€ 4,30 - € 8,80
child (2-6 yrs)	€ 2,00 - € 5,40
dog	€ 2,10 - € 5,80

FRANCE – Hourtin-Plage

Airotel Camping la Côte d'Argent

F-33990 Hourtin-Plage (Gironde)
t: 05 56 09 10 25 e: info@cca33.com
alanrogers.com/FR33110 www.cca33.com

Accommodation: ☑ Pitch ☑ Mobile home/chalet ☑ Hotel/B&B ☐ Apartment

Côte d'Argent is a large, well equipped site for leisurely family holidays. It makes an ideal base for walkers and cyclists with over 100 km. of cycle lanes in the area. Hourtin-Plage is a pleasant invigorating resort on the Atlantic coast and a popular location for watersports enthusiasts. The site's top attraction is its pool complex, where wooden bridges connect the pools and islands and there are sunbathing and play areas plus an indoor heated pool. The site has 588 touring pitches (all with 10A electricity), not always clearly defined, arranged under trees with some on sand. High quality entertainment takes place at the impressive bar/restaurant near the entrance. Spread over 20 hectares of undulating sand-based terrain and in the midst of a pine forest. The site is well organised and ideal for children.

You might like to know

During July and August, archery contests and horse riding are organised for children. There is also a surf school (300 m. away from the campsite) with special activities for children.

- ☑ Multilingual children's club – pre-school
- ☑ Multilingual children's club – 5-10 year olds
- ☑ Multilingual children's club – 10-14 year olds
- ☑ Creative crafts
- ☑ Bicycle hire for children
- ☐ Facilities for children in wash blocks
- ☑ Children's pool
- ☑ Children's play area
- ☐ Crèche and/or babysitting
- ☑ Local information of interest for children

Facilities: Very clean sanitary blocks include provision for disabled visitors. Washing machines. Motorcaravan service points. Large supermarket, restaurant, takeaway, pizzeria, bar (all open 1/6-15/9). Four outdoor pools with slides and flumes (1/6-19/9). Indoor pool (all season). Fitness room. Massage (Institut de Beauté). Tennis. Play areas. Miniclub, organised entertainment in season. Bicycle hire. WiFi (charged). ATM. Charcoal barbecues are not permitted. Hotel (12 rooms). Off site: Path to the beach 300 m. Fishing and riding. Golf 30 km.

Open: 14 May - 18 September.

Directions: Turn off D101 Hourtin-Soulac road 3 km. north of Hourtin. Then join D101E signed Hourtin-Plage. Site is 300 m. from the beach. GPS: 45.22297, -1.16465

Charges guide

Per unit incl. 2 persons and electricity	€ 26,00 - € 48,00
extra person	€ 4,00 - € 8,00
child (3-9 yrs)	€ 3,00 - € 7,00
dog	€ 2,00 - € 6,00

FRANCE – Vias-Plage

Yelloh! Village le Club Farret

F-34450 Vias-Plage (Hérault)
t: 04 67 21 64 45 e: info@yellohvillage-club-farret.com
alanrogers.com/FR34110 www.yellohvillage-club-farret.com

Accommodation: ☑ Pitch ☑ Mobile home/chalet ☐ Hotel/B&B ☐ Apartment

Well maintained and with welcoming, helpful staff, everywhere is neat and tidy. It is
a large, busy site but the atmosphere is very relaxed. There are 710 good sized, level,
grassy pitches, with 340 for touring with 6A electricity. And there is some shade from
many trees. The large heated pool has lots of sunbathing room with a new terrace. The
safe beach is alongside the site so some pitches have sea views. There is a wide range
of entertainments and the activities include an extensive art programme. The restaurant
is high above the pool with views of the sea, everything is open all season. This superb
site of excellent quality has been developed by the Giner family with love and care over
the last 50 years. Activities include pottery, silk painting, mosaics and water colours.
A new spa and wellness centre opened for the 2010 season. The mobile home areas are
very smart and have been attractively landscaped, with African or Balinese themes.
A new area for mobile homes is vehicle free.

You might like to know
There is a wide variety of children's
entertainment on offer here – dance classes,
archery, fitness courses and much more.

☑ Multilingual children's club – pre-school
☑ Multilingual children's club – 5-10 year olds
☑ Multilingual children's club – 10-14 year olds
☑ Creative crafts
☐ Bicycle hire for children
☑ Facilities for children in wash blocks
☑ Children's pool
☑ Children's play area
☐ Crèche and/or babysitting
☑ Local information of interest
  for children

Facilities: Very clean toilet blocks, children's
toilets, baby rooms, facilities for disabled visitors.
Washing machines. Dog shower. Well stocked
supermarket. Hairdresser. Bars with pizzas,
snacks, takeaway. Restaurant. Heated swimming
pool complex (now enlarged to 1,000 sq.m)
with lifeguard all season. New spa and wellness
centre with sauna, jacuzzi etc. Excellent play
area. Miniclub (5-12 yrs). Teenagers' club
(13-17 yrs). Tennis. Archery. Programme
of games. Multisports court. Bicycle hire.
Off site: Riding 1 km. Golf 10 km. Sailing and
windsurfing.

Open: 14 April - 8 October.

Directions: Site is south of Vias at Vias-Plage.
From N112 (Béziers - Agde) take D137 signed
Vias-Plage. Site is signed on the left.
GPS: 43.29103, 3.41912

Charges guide

Per unit incl. 2 persons

and electricity	€ 19,00 - € 47,00
extra person	€ 6,00 - € 8,00
extra tent	€ 3,00
dog	€ 4,00

Camping les Sablines

Chemin des Montilles, Vendres-Plage, F-34350 Vendres (Hérault)
t: 04 67 32 74 29 e: info@homair-vacances.fr
alanrogers.com/FR34320 www.homair-vacances.com

Accommodation: ☑Pitch ☑Mobile home/chalet ☐ Hotel/B&B ☐ Apartment

This is a neat and tidy site with direct access to the beach via a path over the dunes. It is owned by Homair, the French tour operator, and has 186 mobile homes of various sizes to let, with just nine touring pitches. The site is level and attractively landscaped with trees and shrubs, with grass and hedging surrounding the pitches which are linked by tarmac roads. An attractive pool area with slides is overlooked by a bar and restaurant. The site would be a good choice for families with children. The bustling area of Valras Plage is a typical French seaside resort with lots going on. In the main season, a tourist train connects this wonderful stretch of sandy beaches. Sablines is situated to the west, in a quieter area, with a path to the beach and Vendres' newly developed harbour about half a kilometre further on. It is easy to access the A19 if you wish to visit Spain or Andorra.

You might like to know
Miniclub for children aged 6-12 years. Adults will appreciate the many local vineyards and enjoy sampling the wines!

☐ Multilingual children's club – pre-school
☐ Multilingual children's club – 5-10 year olds
☐ Multilingual children's club – 10-14 year olds
☑ Creative crafts
☐ Bicycle hire for children
☐ Facilities for children in wash blocks
☑ Children's pool
☑ Children's play area
☐ Crèche and/or babysitting
☑ Local information of interest
   for children

Facilities: Three toilet blocks of older design. Small shop (bread can be ordered). Restaurant, bar and takeaway (early May-late Sept). Swimming pool with slides and paddling pool area and jacuzzi. Play area. Multisports court. WiFi (charged). Charcoal barbecues are not permitted. Off site: Beach 500 m.

Open: 2 April - 18 September.

Directions: From A9 exit 36 (Béziers Ouest), follow signs for Valras then Campings Plage Ouest and pick up site sign.
GPS: 43.229733, 3.2485

Charges guide

Per unit incl. 2 persons and electricity	€ 15,00 - € 40,00
extra person	€ 9,00 - € 17,00
child (3-6 yrs)	€ 2,50 - € 5,00
dog	€ 3,00

FRANCE – Sonzay

Kawan Village l'Arada Parc

Rue de la Baratière, F-37360 Sonzay (Indre-et-Loire)
t: 02 47 24 72 69   e: info@laradaparc.com
alanrogers.com/FR37060   www.laradaparc.com

Accommodation: ☑Pitch ☑Mobile home/chalet   ☐ Hotel/B&B ☐ Apartment

A good, well maintained site in a quiet location, easy to find from the motorway and popular as an overnight stop. Camping l'Arada Parc is an attractive family site nestling in the heart of the Touranelle countryside between the Loire and Loir valleys. The 73 grass touring pitches all have electricity and 19 have water and drainage. The clearly marked pitches, some slightly sloping, are separated by trees and shrubs, some of which are now providing a degree of shade. An attractive, heated pool is on a pleasant terrace beside the restaurant. Entertainment, themed evenings and activities for children are organised in July/August. This is a new site with modern facilities which include a superb new covered pool and fitness room. The campsite is situated in the heart of 'château country' so you will have the opportunity to visit Villandry, Azay le Rideau and Langeais. Why not try the vineyards too? Chinon, Vouvray, Touraine and Amboise are nearby with plenty of tasting opportunities.

You might like to know
Arada Parc is located at the heart of the Loire château region, and is also close to many of the area's celebrated vineyards.

- ☑ Multilingual children's club – pre-school
- ☑ Multilingual children's club – 5-10 year olds
- ☑ Multilingual children's club – 10-14 year olds
- ☑ Creative crafts
- ☐ Bicycle hire for children
- ☑ Facilities for children in wash blocks
- ☑ Children's pool
- ☑ Children's play area
- ☐ Crèche and/or babysitting
- ☑ Local information of interest for children

Facilities: Two modern toilet blocks provide unisex toilets, showers and washbasins in cubicles. Baby room. Facilities for disabled visitors (wheelchair users may find the gravel access difficult). Laundry facilities. Shop, bar, restaurant and takeaway. Motorcaravan service. Outdoor swimming pool (no Bermuda-style shorts; 1/5-15/9). Heated, covered pool. Fitness room. Small play area. Games area. Boules. TV room. Bicycle hire. Internet access. WiFi throughout site. Footpath to village. Off site: Tennis 200 m. Fishing 500 m. Golf 12 km. Riding 14 km.

Open: 26 March - 1 November.

Directions: Sonzay is northwest of Tours. From the new A28 north of Tours take the exit to Neuillé-Pont-Pierre which is on the N138 Le Mans - Tours road. Then take D766 towards Château la Vallière and turn southwest to Sonzay. Follow signs. GPS: 47.625963, 0.452843

Charges guide

Per unit incl. 2 persons and electricity (10A)	€ 19,00 - € 25,10
extra person	€ 4,00 - € 5,30
child (2-10 yrs)	free - € 3,80
dog	€ 1,50 - € 2,00

FRANCE – Vielle-Saint-Girons

Camping Club International Eurosol

Route de la Plage, F-40560 Vielle-Saint-Girons (Landes)
t: 05 58 47 90 14 e: contact@camping-eurosol.com
alanrogers.com/FR40060 www.camping-eurosol.com

Accommodation: ☑Pitch ☑Mobile home/chalet ☐ Hotel/B&B ☐ Apartment

Eurosol is an attractive, friendly and well maintained site extending over 15 hectares of undulating ground amongst mature pine trees giving good shade. Of the 356 touring pitches, 209 have electricity (10A) with 120 fully serviced. A wide range of mobile homes and chalets are available for rent too (no dogs). This is very much a family site with multilingual entertainers. Many games and tournaments are organised and a beach volleyball competition is held regularly in front of the bar. The adjacent boules terrain is also floodlit. An excellent sandy beach 700 m. from the site has supervised bathing in high season, and is ideal for surfing. The landscaped swimming pool complex is impressive with three large pools, one of which is covered and heated, and a large children's paddling pool. There is a convivial restaurant and takeaway food service. A large supermarket is well stocked with fresh bread daily and international newspapers. A number of cycle trails lead from the site through the vast forests of Les Landes.

You might like to know

The sandy beach lying just 700 m. from the site is regarded as one of the largest and most beautiful in the southwest of France.

☐ Multilingual children's club – pre-school
☑ Multilingual children's club – 5-10 year olds
☐ Multilingual children's club – 10-14 year olds
☑ Creative crafts
☑ Bicycle hire for children
☑ Facilities for children in wash blocks
☑ Children's pool
☑ Children's play area
☐ Crèche and/or babysitting
☑ Local information of interest for children

Facilities: Four main toilet blocks and two smaller blocks are comfortable and clean with facilities for babies and disabled visitors. Motorcaravan services. Fridge rental. Well stocked shop and bar (all season). Restaurant, takeaway (2/6-8/9). Stage for live shows arranged in July/Aug. Outdoor swimming pool, paddling pool (all season) and heated covered pool (low season). Tennis. Multisports court. Bicycle hire. WiFi (charged). Charcoal barbecues are not permitted. Off site: Riding (July/Aug) 200 m. Surf school 500 m. Beach and fishing 700 m. Golf 18 km.

Open: 19 May - 15 September.

Directions: Turn off D652 at St Girons on the D42 towards St Girons-Plage. Site is on left before coming to beach (4.5 km).
GPS: 43.95166, -1.35212

Charges guide

Per unit incl. 2 persons and electricity	€ 18,00 - € 36,00
extra person (over 4 yrs)	€ 5,00
dog	€ 4,00

Camping du Domaine de la Rive

Route de Bordeaux, F-40600 Biscarrosse (Landes)
t: 05 58 78 12 33 e: info@lafive.fr
alanrogers.com/FR40100 www.larive.fr

Accommodation: ☑Pitch ☑Mobile home/chalet ☐ Hotel/B&B ☐ Apartment

Surrounded by pine woods, la Rive has a superb beach-side location on Lac de Sanguinet. It provides 250 mostly level, numbered and clearly defined touring pitches of 100 sq.m. all with electricity connections (10A). The swimming pool complex is wonderful with pools linked by water channels and bridges. There is also a jacuzzi, paddling pool and two large swimming pools all surrounded by sunbathing areas and decorated with palm trees. An indoor pool is heated and open all season. The latest additions are a super children's aquapark with various games, and a top quality bar/restaurant complex where regular entertainment is organised. The beach is excellent, shelving gently to provide safe bathing for all ages. There are windsurfers and small craft can be launched from the site's slipway. This is a friendly site with a good mix of nationalities.

You might like to know

The campsite has a skate park, a bouncy castle and a secure field where children can play safely. There is a small children's garden too.

- ☑ Multilingual children's club – pre-school
- ☑ Multilingual children's club – 5-10 year olds
- ☑ Multilingual children's club – 10-14 year olds
- ☑ Creative crafts
- ☐ Bicycle hire for children
- ☑ Facilities for children in wash blocks
- ☑ Children's pool
- ☑ Children's play area
- ☐ Crèche and/or babysitting
- ☑ Local information of interest for children

Facilities: Five good clean toilet blocks have washbasins in cabins and mainly British style toilets. Facilities for disabled visitors. Baby baths. Motorcaravan service point. Shop with gas. New bar/restaurant complex with entertainment. Swimming pool complex (supervised July/Aug). Games room. Play area. Tennis. Bicycle hire. Boules. Archery. Fishing. Watersports equipment hire. Waterskiing. Tournaments (June-Aug). Skateboard park. Trampolines. Miniclub. No charcoal barbecues on pitches. WiFi (charged). Off site: Riding 2 km. Golf 8 km. Beach 17 km.

Open: 6 April - 9 September.

Directions: Take D652 from Sanguinet to Biscarrosse and site is signed on the right in about 6 km. Turn right and follow tarmac road for 2 km. GPS: 44.46052, -1.13065

Charges guide

Per unit incl. 2 persons and electricity	€ 24,50 - € 47,00
extra person	€ 3,80 - € 8,50
child (3-7 yrs)	€ 2,50 - € 7,00
dog	€ 5,00 - € 7,00

FRANCE – Pierrefitte-sur-Sauldre

Leading Camping les Alicourts

Domaine des Alicourts, F-41300 Pierrefitte-sur-Sauldre (Loir-et-Cher)
t: **02 54 88 63 34** e: **info@lesalicourts.com**
alanrogers.com/FR41030 www.lesalicourts.com

Accommodation: ☑ Pitch ☑ Mobile home/chalet ☐ Hotel/B&B ☐ Apartment

A secluded holiday village set in the heart of the forest, with many sporting facilities and a super spa centre, les Alicourts is midway between Orléans and Bourges, to the east of the A71. There are 490 pitches, 150 for touring and the remainder occupied by mobile homes and chalets. All pitches have 6A electricity and good provision for water, and most are 150 sq.m. (min. 100 sq.m.). Locations vary, from wooded to more open areas, thus giving a choice of amount of shade. All facilities are open all season and the leisure amenities are exceptional. The Senseo Balnéo centre offers indoor pools, hydrotherapy, massage and spa treatments for over 18s only (some special family sessions are provided). An inviting outdoor water complex (all season) includes two pools, a pool with a wave machine and a beach area, not forgetting three water slides. Competitions and activities are organised for adults and children including a high season club for children and a dance for adults. A member of Leading Campings Group.

You might like to know

There is a mini disco for children every evening, and during high season they are kept entertained by shows – including one they can star in themselves!

☐ Multilingual children's club – pre-school
☑ Multilingual children's club – 5-10 year olds
☑ Multilingual children's club – 10-14 year olds
☐ Creative crafts
☑ Bicycle hire for children
☑ Facilities for children in wash blocks
☑ Children's pool
☑ Children's play area
☐ Crèche and/or babysitting
☐ Local information of interest
   for children

Facilities: Three modern sanitary blocks include some washbasins in cabins and baby bathrooms. Laundry facilities. Facilities for disabled visitors. Motorcaravan services. Shop. Restaurant. Takeaway in bar with terrace. Pool complex. Spa centre. 7-hectare lake (fishing, bathing, canoes, pedaloes). 9-hole golf course. Adventure play area. Tennis. Minigolf. Boules. Roller skating/skateboarding (bring own equipment). Bicycle hire. Internet access and WiFi (charged).

Open: 29 April - 9 September.

Directions: From A71, take Lamotte Beuvron exit (no. 3) or from N20 Orléans to Vierzon turn left on to D923 towards Aubigny. After 14 km. turn right at camping sign on to D24E. Site signed in 4 km. GPS: 47.54398, 2.19193

Charges guide

Per unit incl. 2 persons and electricity	€ 20,00 - € 44,00
extra person	€ 7,00 - € 10,00
child (5-17 yrs)	€ 6,00 - € 8,00
child (1-4yrs)	free - € 6,00
dog	€ 5,00 - € 7,00

Kawan Village du Deffay

B.P. 18 Le Deffay, Sainte Reine-de-Bretagne, F-44160 Pontchâteau (Loire-Atlantique)
t: **02 40 88 00 57** e: **campingdudeffay@wanadoo.fr**
alanrogers.com/FR44090 www.camping-le-deffay.com

Accommodation: ☑ Pitch ☑ Mobile home/chalet ☑ Hotel/B&B ☐ Apartment

A family managed site, Château du Deffay is a refreshing departure from the usual formula in that it is not over organised and supervised and has no tour operator units. The 170 good sized, fairly level pitches have pleasant views and are either on open grass, on shallow terraces divided by hedges, or informally arranged in a central, slightly sloping wooded area. Most have electricity (6/10A). The bar, restaurant and covered pool are located within the old courtyard area of the smaller château that dates from before 1400. A significant attraction of the site is the large, unfenced lake which is well stocked for fishermen and even has free pedaloes for children. The landscape is wonderfully natural and the site blends well with the rural environment of the estate, lake and farmland which surround it. Alpine type chalets overlook the lake and fit in well with the environment and the larger château (built 1880 and now offering B&B) stands slightly away from the camping area but provides a wonderful backdrop for a stroll.

You might like to know

Why not take part in one of the themed treks (nature, trees etc) through the beautiful local countryside?

☐ Multilingual children's club – pre-school
☐ Multilingual children's club – 5-10 year olds
☐ Multilingual children's club – 10-14 year olds
☑ Creative crafts
☐ Bicycle hire for children
☐ Facilities for children in wash blocks
☑ Children's pool
☑ Children's play area
☐ Crèche and/or babysitting
☑ Local information of interest
   for children

Facilities: The main toilet block is well maintained, if a little dated, and is well equipped including washbasins in cabins, provision for disabled visitors, and a baby bathroom. Laundry facilities. Shop. Bar and small restaurant with takeaway (1/5-15/9). Covered and heated swimming pool (at 28 degrees when we visited) and paddling pool (all season). Play area. TV. Entertainment in season including miniclub. Fishing and pedaloes on the lake. Torches useful. WiFi (charged). Off site: Golf 7 km. Riding 10 km. Beach 25 km.

Open: 1 May - 30 September.

Directions: Site is signed from the D33 Pontchâteau - Herbignac road near Ste Reine. Also signed from the D773 and N165-E60 (exit 13). GPS: 47.44106, -2.15981

Charges guide

Per unit incl. 2 persons and electricity	€ 18,30 - € 28,20
extra person	€ 3,35 - € 5,60
child (2-12 yrs)	€ 2,30 - € 3,90

Camping le Patisseau

29 rue du Patisseau, F-44210 Pornic (Loire-Atlantique)
t: 02 40 82 10 39 e: contact@lepatisseau.com
alanrogers.com/FR44100 www.lepatisseau.com

Accommodation: ☑ Pitch ☑ Mobile home/chalet ☐ Hotel/B&B ☐ Apartment

Le Patisseau is situated in the countryside just a short drive from the fishing village of Pornic. It is a relaxed site with a large number of mobile homes and chalets, and popular with young families and teenagers. The 102 touring pitches, all with electrical connections (6A), are divided between the attractive 'forest' area with plenty of shade from mature trees and the more open 'prairie' area. Some are on a slight slope and access to others might be tricky for larger units. A railway runs along the bottom half of the site with trains several times a day, (but none overnight) and the noise is minimal. The Morice family work very hard to maintain a friendly atmosphere. The site's spacious restaurant and bar overlook the indoor pool. Outside two waterslides are cleverly concealed amongst the trees. A number of communal barbecues are provided throughout the site, helping to create a sociable atmosphere.

Special offers
Discounted entry fees to the animal park (20 km) and the sealife centre (30 km).

You might like to know
The beach is just 2.5 km. away, but there's plenty to do on site – a children's club, three playgrounds, a heated indoor pool with a paddling pool, and an outdoor swimming complex with slides, paddling pool and water games. Why not round off the day with one of Pornic's delicious ice creams, available during the strawberry picking season?

☐ Multilingual children's club – pre-school
☑ Multilingual children's club – 5-10 year olds
☐ Multilingual children's club – 10-14 year olds
☑ Creative crafts
☐ Bicycle hire for children
☑ Facilities for children in wash blocks
☑ Children's pool
☑ Children's play area
☐ Crèche and/or babysitting
☑ Local information of interest for children

Facilities: The modern heated toilet block is very spacious and well fitted; some open style washbasins, controllable showers in large cubicles with washbasins. Good facilities for disabled visitors and babies. Laundry rooms. Shop (1/7-30/8). Bar, restaurant and takeaway. Indoor heated pool with sauna, jacuzzi and spa. Small heated outdoor pools and water slides (1/6-30/9). Play area. Multisports court. Bicycle hire. WiFi. Off site: Fishing and beach 2.5 km. Riding, golf, sailing and boat launching all 5 km.

Open: 3 April - 11 November.

Directions: Pornic is 19 km. south of the St Nazaire bridge. Access to site is at junction of the D751 Nantes - Pornic road with the D213 St Nazaire - Noirmoutier 'Route Bleue'. From north take exit for D751 Nantes. From south follow D751 Clion-sur-Mer. At roundabout north of D213 take exit for le Patisseau and follow signs to site. Avoid Pornic town centre. GPS: 47.118833, -2.072833

Charges guide

Per unit incl. 2 persons and electricity (6A)	€ 25,00 - € 41,00
extra person	€ 4,00 - € 8,00
child (under 7 yrs)	€ 3,00 - € 5,00
dog	€ 6,00

Camping le Fief

57 chemin du Fief, F-44250 Saint Brévin-les-Pins (Loire-Atlantique)
t: 02 40 27 23 86   e: camping@lefief.com
alanrogers.com/FR44190   www.lefief.com

Accommodation: ☑Pitch   ☑Mobile home/chalet   ☑Hotel/B&B   ☐ Apartment

If you are a family with young children or lively teenagers, this could be the campsite for you. Le Fief is a well established site only 800 m. from sandy beaches on the southern Brittany coast. It has a magnificent aquapark with outdoor and covered swimming pools, paddling pools, slides, river rapids, fountains, jets and more. The site has 174 pitches for touring units (out of 405). Whilst these all have 5A electricity, they vary in size and many are worn and may be untidy. There are also 183 mobile homes and chalets to rent and 48 privately-owned units. This is a lively site in high season with a variety of entertainment and organised activity for all ages. This ranges from a miniclub for 5-12 year olds, to Tonic Days in a state-of-the-art wellness centre with aquagym, jogging and sports competitions, and to evening events which include karaoke, themed dinners and cabaret. There are plenty of sporting facilities for active youngsters.

You might like to know

You can choose between the great pool complex on site, or the sea, just 800 m. away, with its brilliant sandy beach.

- ☑ Multilingual children's club – pre-school
- ☑ Multilingual children's club – 5-10 year olds
- ☑ Multilingual children's club – 10-14 year olds
- ☑ Creative crafts
- ☑ Bicycle hire for children
- ☐ Facilities for children in wash blocks
- ☑ Children's pool
- ☑ Children's play area
- ☐ Crèche and/or babysitting
- ☑ Local information of interest for children

Facilities: One excellent new toilet block and three others of a lower standard. Laundry facilities. Shop (1/6-31/8). Bar, restaurant and takeaway (3/4-26/9) with terrace overlooking the pool complex. Outdoor pools, etc. (1/5-15/9). Covered pool (all season). Wellness centre. Play area. Tennis. Pétanque. Archery. Games room. Internet access. Organised entertainment and activities (weekends April/June, daily July/Aug). Bicycle hire. Off site: Beach 800 m. Bus stop 1 km. Riding 1 km. Golf 15 km. Planète Sauvage safari park.

Open: 3 April - 3 October.

Directions: From the St Nazaire bridge take the fourth exit from the D213 signed St Brévin-l'Océan. Continue over first roundabout and bear right at the second to join Chemin du Fief. The site is on the right, well signed.
GPS: 47.23486, -2.16757

Charges guide

Per unit incl. 2 persons and electricity	€ 22,00 - € 45,00
extra person	€ 5,00 - € 10,00
child (0-7 yrs)	€ 2,50 - € 5,00
dog	€ 3,00 - € 8,00

No credit cards.

Kawan Village les Bois du Bardelet

Route de Bourges, Le Petit Bardelet, F-45500 Gien (Loiret)
t: 02 38 67 47 39 e: contact@bardelet.com
alanrogers.com/FR45010 www.bardelet.com

Accommodation: ☑ Pitch ☑ Mobile home/chalet ☐ Hotel/B&B ☐ Apartment

This attractive, high quality and lively site, ideal for families with young children, is in a rural setting and well situated for exploring the less well known eastern part of the Loire Valley. Two lakes (one for boating, one for fishing) and a pool complex have been attractively landscaped in 12 hectares of former farmland, blending old and new with natural wooded areas and more open field areas with rural views. There are 260 large, level grass pitches with 130 for touring units. All have 8/16A electricity, 20 have water and waste water and some have hardstanding. The communal areas are based in attractively converted former farm buildings with a wide range of leisure facilities. A weekly family club card can be purchased to make use of the many activities on a daily basis (some high season only). Excursions are organised to Paris, famous châteaux and vineyards plus several riverboat trips. The site is an easy cycle ride from the nearest town of Gien which has a range of shops, bars, restaurants and museums.

You might like to know

Close to site you can try your hand at paragliding and enjoy breathtaking views of the surrounding countryside from the air.

- ☑ Multilingual children's club – pre-school
- ☑ Multilingual children's club – 5-10 year olds
- ☑ Multilingual children's club – 10-14 year olds
- ☑ Creative crafts
- ☑ Bicycle hire for children
- ☑ Facilities for children in wash blocks
- ☑ Children's pool
- ☑ Children's play area
- ☐ Crèche and/or babysitting
- ☑ Local information of interest for children

Facilities: Two toilet blocks include facilities for disabled visitors and babies. Washing machines, dryers. Shop (1/4-11/9). Bar. Snack bar, takeaway (all 1/4-11/9). Full restaurant (high season and weekends). Heated outdoor pool (1/5-31/8). Heated indoor pool and children's pool with purchased club card (1/4-11/9). Aquagym, fitness and jacuzzi room. Games area. Archery. Canoeing and fishing. Tennis. Minigolf. Boules. Bicycle hire. Playground. WiFi (charged). Off site: Supermarket 5 km. Riding 7 km. Golf 25 km. Walking and cycling routes.

Open: 1 April - 30 September.

Directions: Leave A77 autoroute (exit 19 Gien). Take D940 (signed Bourges) to Gien, cross river Loire, continue D940 for 5 km. At junction with D53 (site signed) turn right and right again to cross D940 (no left turn). Follow signs for 1.5 km. to site. GPS: 47.64152, 2.61528

Charges guide

Per unit incl. 2 persons and electricity	€ 24,00 - € 32,00
extra person	€ 4,90 - € 6,50
child (2-5 yrs)	free - € 6,50
dog	€ 4,00

FRANCE – Ravenoville-Plage

Kawan Village le Cormoran

2 le Cormoran, F-50480 Ravenoville-Plage (Manche)
t: 02 33 41 33 94   e: lecormoran@wanadoo.fr
alanrogers.com/FR50050   www.lecormoran.com

Accommodation: ☑ Pitch ☑ Mobile home/chalet ☐ Hotel/B&B ☐ Apartment

This welcoming, environmentally friendly, family run site, close to Cherbourg and Caen, is situated just across the road from a long sandy beach. It is also close to Utah beach and is ideally located for those wishing to visit the many museums, landing beaches and remembrance gardens of WW2. On flat, quite open ground, the site has 110 good size pitches on level grass, all with 6/10A electricity (Europlug). Some extra large pitches are available. The well kept pitches are separated by mature hedges and the site is decorated with flowering shrubs. A covered pool, a sauna and a gym are among recent improvements. These facilities, plus a shop, comfortable bar and takeaway are open all season. This modern, clean and fresh looking campsite caters for both families and couples and would be ideal for a holiday in this interesting area of France. There are many small towns in the area and in early June, you may find historical groups re-enacting battles and the events of 1944-1945.

You might like to know

Le Cormoran, on the Normandy landing beaches, is a paradise for children and parents alike. There is plenty to do and see – bouncy castles, trampolines, go-karting, horse riding (in summer), indoor pool and paddling pool, and goats' corner.

☐ Multilingual children's club – pre-school
☑ Multilingual children's club – 5-10 year olds
☑ Multilingual children's club – 10-14 year olds
☑ Creative crafts
☑ Bicycle hire for children
☑ Facilities for children in wash blocks
☑ Children's pool
☑ Children's play area
☐ Crèche and/or babysitting
☑ Local information of interest for children

Facilities: Four toilet blocks, three heated, are maintained to a good standard. Laundry facilities. Shop. Bar and terrace. Snacks and takeaway. Outdoor pool (1/6-15/9, unsupervised). New covered pool, sauna and gym (all season). Play areas. Tennis. Boules. Entertainment, TV and games room. Billiard golf. Playing field with archery (July/Aug). Hairdresser and masseuse. Bicycle and shrimp net hire. Riding (July/Aug). Communal barbecues. BMX parc for children. WiFi (charged). Off site: Beach 20 m. Sand yachting. Golf (9 holes) 3 km. Ste-Mère-Eglise - famous for the paratrooper suspended from the church tower, has many museums and annual D-Day celebrations in June 9 km.

Open: 7 April - 29 September.

Directions: From N13 take Ste Mère-Eglise exit and in centre of town take road to Ravenoville (6 km), then Ravenoville-Plage (3 km). Just before beach turn right and site is 500 m.
GPS: 49.46643, -1.23533

Charges guide

Per unit incl. 2 persons and electricity	€ 21,00 - € 33,00
extra person	€ 4,00 - € 7,90
child (5-10 yrs)	€ 2,00 - € 3,00
dog	€ 3,00

FRANCE – Bidart

Castel le Ruisseau des Pyrénées

Route d'Arbonne, F-64210 Bidart (Pyrénées-Atlantiques)
t: 05 59 41 94 50 e: francoise.dumont3@wanadoo.fr
alanrogers.com/FR64070 www.camping-le-ruisseau.fr

Accommodation: ☑ Pitch ☑ Mobile home/chalet ☐ Hotel/B&B ☐ Apartment

This busy site, with a large play area filled with equipment is ideal for young families. It is about 2 km. from Bidart and 2.5 km. from a sandy beach. There are two swimming pools with slides on the main site, and across the road an indoor heated pool and new spa complex (charged in July/August) with outdoor fitness equipment. Pitches on the main campsite are individual, marked and of a good size, either on flat terraces or around the lake. The terrain is wooded so the great majority of them have some shade. Electrical connections are available throughout. The site has a number of steep slopes to negotiate. Entertainment is provided in the main season, with organised day-time sports and evening entertainment nightly in season. The site is popular with tour operators and the site has a number of its own mobile homes. There is also a little lake where fishing is possible, in the area at the bottom of the site which has a very pleasant open aspect and includes a large play area.

You might like to know
The Pays Basque is a wonderful region between mountains and sea. Camping Le Ruisseau runs a free shuttle bus to a sandy beach (in high season).

- ☐ Multilingual children's club – pre-school
- ☑ Multilingual children's club – 5-10 year olds
- ☑ Multilingual children's club – 10-14 year olds
- ☐ Creative crafts
- ☑ Bicycle hire for children
- ☐ Facilities for children in wash blocks
- ☑ Children's pool
- ☑ Children's play area
- ☐ Crèche and/or babysitting
- ☑ Local information of interest for children

Facilities: Two main blocks and some extra smaller units. Washing machines. Motorcaravan service point. Shop, large self-service restaurant with takeaway and bar with terraces, and TV (all 22/5-4/9). Outdoor swimming pools, indoor heated pool and spa complex (all season). Sauna. Large play area. Two tennis courts (free outside July/Aug). Fitness track. TV and games rooms. Minigolf. Bicycle hire. Fishing. Small animal sanctuary. WiFi throughout (charged). Off site: Riding and golf 3 km.

Open: 7 April - 18 September.

Directions: Site is east of Bidart on a minor road towards Arbonne. From A63 autoroute take Biarritz exit (4), turn towards St Jean-de-Luz and Bidart on N10. After Intermarché turn left at roundabout and follow signs to site. GPS: 43.4367, -1.5677

Charges guide

Per unit incl. 2 persons and electricity	€ 19,00 - € 44,00
extra person	€ 5,00 - € 7,00
child (under 7 yrs)	€ 3,50 - € 5,00
dog	free - € 4,00

Kawan Village Caravaning Ma Prairie

1 avenue des Coteaux, F-66140 Canet-en-Roussillon (Pyrénées-Orientales)
t: 04 68 73 26 17 e: ma.prairie@wanadoo.fr
alanrogers.com/FR66020 www.maprairie.com

Accommodation: ☑Pitch ☑Mobile home/chalet ☐ Hotel/B&B ☐ Apartment

Ma Prairie is an excellent site and its place in this guide goes back over 30 years. Then it was simply a field surrounded by vineyards. The trees planted then have now matured and more continue to be planted, along with colourful shrubs providing a comfortable, park-like setting with some 200 touring pitches, all with electricity and 15 with water and drainage. There are also 50 mobile homes available to rent and 10 privately owned. It is a peaceful haven some 3 km. back from the sea but within walking distance of Canet village itself. The Gil family provide a warm welcome and reception boasts an impressive international collection of hats, helmets and uniform caps. The restaurant and bar is across the road and overlooks a modern, attractive pool complex and wonderful old palm tree. Today there is Internet access, some mobile homes and modern housing has crept up but there are still vineyards close and the wine sold in reception is from the family vineyard.

Special offers
Children under 3 go free all season. Children under 9 go free before 7 July and after 18 August.

You might like to know
Special dance evenings for children are held every Friday in July and August.

- ☐ Multilingual children's club – pre-school
- ☑ Multilingual children's club – 5-10 year olds
- ☐ Multilingual children's club – 10-14 year olds
- ☑ Creative crafts
- ☐ Bicycle hire for children
- ☐ Facilities for children in wash blocks
- ☑ Children's pool
- ☑ Children's play area
- ☐ Crèche and/or babysitting
- ☑ Local information of interest for children

Facilities: Fully equipped toilet blocks, baby bath. Washing machines and dryers. No shop but bread can be ordered. Covered snack bar and takeaway. Air-conditioned bar and restaurant. Large adult pool, splendid children's pool. Multisports court. TV. Amusement machines. Daily activity and entertainment programme in season including dancing and live music once a week. WiFi available over most of the site and Internet access is available in reception. Off site: Supermarket 400 m. Riding 600 m. Sandy beach 3 km. Golf 6 km. Canet Village within walking distance with all amenities. Bus/tram services to Canet Plage.

Open: 5 May - 25 September.

Directions: Leave autoroute A9 at Perpignan North towards Barcarès. Site access is from the D11 Perpignan road (exit 5), close to the junction with D617 in Canet-Village. Go under bridge, right at roundabout then left to site. GPS: 42.70135, 2.99968

Charges guide

Per unit incl. 2 persons and electricity	€ 21,50 - € 38,50
extra person	€ 4,00 - € 7,50
child (4-9 yrs)	free - € 6,00
dog	free - € 3,00

FRANCE – Canet-en-Roussillon

Yelloh! Village le Brasilia

B.P. 204, F-66141 Canet-en-Roussillon (Pyrénées-Orientales)
t: 04 68 80 23 82 e: info@lebrasilia.fr
alanrogers.com/FR66070 www.brasilia.fr

Accommodation: ☑ Pitch ☑ Mobile home/chalet ☐ Hotel/B&B ☐ Apartment

Situated across the yacht harbour from the upmarket resort of Canet-Plage, le Brasilia is an impressive, well managed family site directly beside the beach. It is pretty, neat and well kept with an amazingly wide range of facilities – indeed, it is camping at its best. There are 428 neatly hedged touring pitches, all with electricity (6-10A) and 315 with water and drainage. They vary in size from 80 to 120 sq.m. and some of the longer pitches are suitable for two families together. With a range of shade from pines and flowering shrubs, less on pitches near the beach, there are neat access roads (sometimes narrow for large units). There are also 161 pitches with mobile homes or chalets to rent (the new ones have their own gardens). The sandy beach here is busy, with a beach club (you can hire windsurfing boards). A completely new pool complex is planned with pools catering for all ages and hydrotherapy facilities for adults. A member of Yelloh! Village and Leading Campings Group.

You might like to know
Spain is very close and day trips to towns such as Figueras (Dali Museum), Girona or even Barcelona are possible.

- ☑ Multi-lingual children's club – pre-school
- ☑ Multi-lingual children's club – 5-10 year olds
- ☑ Multi-lingual children's club – 10-14 year olds
- ☑ Creative crafts
- ☑ Bicycle hire for children
- ☑ Facilities for children in wash blocks
- ☑ Children's pool
- ☑ Children's play area
- ☐ Crèche and/or babysitting
- ☑ Local information of interest for children

Facilities: Ten modern sanitary blocks are very well equipped and maintained, with British style WCs (some Turkish) and washbasins in cabins. Good facilities for children and disabled visitors. Laundry room. Motorcaravan services. Range of shops. Gas supplies. Bars and restaurant. New pool complex (heated). Play areas. Sports field. Tennis. Sporting activities. Library, games and video room. Hairdresser. Internet café and WiFi. Daily entertainment programme. Bicycle hire. Fishing. ATM. Exchange facilities. Post office. Only gas or electric barbecues are allowed. Off site: Boat launchng and sailing 500 m. Riding 5 km. Golf 12 km.

Open: 21 April - 29 September.

Directions: From A9 exit 41 (Perpignan Centre, Rivesaltes) follow signs for Le Barcarès and Canet on D83 for 10 km. then for Canet (D81). At first Canet roundabout, turn fully back on yourself (Sainte-Marie) and watch for Brasilia sign almost immediately on right. GPS: 42.70467, 3.03483

Charges guide

Per unit incl. 2 persons and electricity (6A)	€ 23,00 - € 55,00
extra person	€ 6,00 - € 9,00
child (3-6 yrs)	free - € 8,50
dog (max. 2)	€ 4,00

Camping l'Hippocampe

Route de Taxo á la Mer, F-66702 Argelès-sur-Mer (Pyrénées-Orientales)
t: **04 68 81 04 61** e: **contact@camping-lasirene.fr**
alanrogers.com/FR66570 www.camping-lasirene.fr

Accommodation: ☑Pitch ☑Mobile home/chalet ☐ Hotel/B&B ☐ Apartment

A sister site to la Sirène just opposite, this site has some touring pitches along with 170 mobile home and chalet pitches and is aimed at families with young children and adults looking for a quieter site. The mobile homes and chalets are all modern, well maintained and have space around them to provide privacy. The pool on site is dedicated to the smaller children and is a great place for them to gain confidence in the water whilst still being able to play. Entertainment, shops, bars and the full range of activities offered by la Sirène, just across the road. Visitors here also have free access to the beach club Emeraude which offers free transport to Plage Nord where the club is situated, complete with bar and snacks.

You might like to know
This is a 'camping kids' site, with free cot, high chair and baby bath.

- ☐ Multilingual children's club – pre-school
- ☑ Multilingual children's club – 5-10 year olds
- ☑ Multilingual children's club – 10-14 year olds
- ☑ Creative crafts
- ☑ Bicycle hire for children
- ☑ Facilities for children in wash blocks
- ☑ Children's pool
- ☑ Children's play area
- ☐ Crèche and/or babysitting
- ☑ Local information of interest for children

Facilities: Pool and laundry. Shop, small bar (all season). All other facilities are at la Sirène just across the road. Riding. Bicycle hire. Off site: Karting, 10-pin bowling, amusement park within 1 km. Beach at Argelès-sur-Mer within 2 km. Fishing 4 km. Golf 7 km.

Open: 17 April - 26 September.

Directions: Leave A9 junction 42. Take the D114, Argelès road. Leave D114 exit 10, follow signs for Plage Nord. Site signed after the first roundabout, on left 2 km. after last roundabout. GPS: 42.5705, 3.03065

Charges guide

Per unit incl. 1-3 persons and electricity	€ 26,00 - € 43,00
extra person	€ 6,00 - € 9,00
child (under 5 yrs)	€ 4,00 - € 6,00
dog	free

FRANCE – Moyenneville

Camping le Val de Trie

Rue des Sources, Bouillancourt-sous-Miannay, F-80870 Moyenneville (Somme)
t: 03 22 31 48 88 e: raphael@camping-levaldetrie.fr
alanrogers.com/FR80060 www.camping-levaldetrie.fr

Accommodation: ☑Pitch ☑Mobile home/chalet ☐ Hotel/B&B ☐ Apartment

Le Val de Trie is a natural countryside site in woodland, near a small village. The 100 numbered, grassy pitches are of a good size, divided by hedges and shrubs with mature trees providing good shade in most areas, and all have electricity (6A) and water. It can be very quiet in April, June, September and October. If there is no-one on site, just choose a pitch or call at the farm to book in. This is maturing into a well managed site with modern facilities and a friendly, relaxed atmosphere. It is well situated for the coast and also the cities of Amiens and Abbeville. There are good walks around the area and a notice board keeps campers up to date with local market, shopping and activity news. English is spoken. The owners of le Val de Trie have recently opened a new campsite nearby, le Clos Cacheleux, where larger units can be accommodated.

You might like to know
Young children will love the farm (they are allowed to feed the cows and goats), and the pony rides.

- ☑ Multilingual children's club – pre-school
- ☐ Multilingual children's club – 5-10 year olds
- ☐ Multilingual children's club – 10-14 year olds
- ☑ Creative crafts
- ☐ Bicycle hire for children
- ☑ Facilities for children in wash blocks
- ☑ Children's pool
- ☑ Children's play area
- ☐ Crèche and/or babysitting
- ☑ Local information of interest for children

Facilities: Two clean, recently renovated sanitary buildings include washbasins in cubicles, units for disabled visitors, babies and children. Laundry facilities. Microwave. Shop (from 1/4), bread to order and butcher visits in season. Bar with TV, snack bar with takeaway (23/4-4/9). Room above bar for children. Covered heated swimming pool with jacuzzi (15/4-30/9). Outdoor pool for children (26/4-10/9). WiFi in bar area (free). Off site: Riding 4 km. Golf 10 km. Beach 12 km.

Open: 1 April - 15 October.

Directions: From A28 take exit 2 near Abbeville and D925 to Miannay. Turn left on D86 to Bouillancourt-sous-Miannay: site is signed in village. GPS: 50.08539, 1.71499

Charges guide

Per unit incl. 2 persons and electricity	€ 18,50 - € 25,80
extra person	€ 3,10 - € 5,30
child (under 7 yrs)	€ 1,90 - € 3,30
dog	€ 1,80 - € 2,00

FRANCE – Fréjus

Camping la Baume – la Palmeraie

3775 rue des Combattants d'Afrique du Nord, F-83618 Fréjus (Var)
t: 04 94 19 88 88   e: reception@labaume-lapalmeraie.com
alanrogers.com/FR83060   www.labaume-lapalmeraie.com

Accommodation: ☑Pitch ☑Mobile home/chalet ☐ Hotel/B&B ☐ Apartment

La Baume is a large, busy site about 5.5 km. from the long sandy beach of Fréjus-Plage, although with its fine and varied selection of swimming pools many people do not bother to make the trip. The pools with their palm trees are remarkable for their size and variety (water slides, etc) – the very large 'feature' pool being a highlight. There is also an aquatic play area and two indoor pools with a slide and a spa area. The site has nearly 250 adequately sized, fully serviced pitches with some separators and most have shade. Although tents are accepted, the site concentrates mainly on caravanning. It becomes full in season. Adjoining la Baume is its sister site, la Palmeraie, providing self-catering accommodation, its own landscaped pool and some entertainment to supplement that at la Baume. There are 500 large pitches for mobile homes. La Baume's convenient location has its downside as there is traffic noise on some pitches from the nearby autoroute – but we soon failed to notice it.

Facilities: Seven toilet blocks. Supermarket, several shops. Two bars, terrace overlooking pools, TV. Restaurant, takeaway. Six swimming pools (heated all season, two covered, plus steam room and jacuzzi). Fitness centre. Tennis. Archery (July/Aug). Skateboard park. Organised events, daytime and evening entertainment, some in English. Amphitheatre. Discos all season. Children's club (all season). 2 play areas renovated. Off site: Bus to Fréjus passes gate. Riding 2 km. Fishing 3 km. Golf and beach 5 km.

Open: 27 March - 25 September
(with full services).

Directions: From west, A8, exit Fréjus, take the N7 southwest (Fréjus). After 4 km, turn left on the D4 and site is 3 km. From east, A8, exit 38 Fréjus and follow signs for Cais. Site is signed.
GPS: 43.45998, 6.72048

Charges guide

Per unit incl. 2 persons, electricity, water/drainage	€ 19,00 - € 45,00
extra person	€ 5,00 - € 13,00
child (under 7 yrs)	free - € 7,00
dog	€ 4,00 - € 5,00

Minimum stay for motorcaravans 2 nights.

You might like to know

The children's club is open Monday to Friday (Sunday afternoons for enrolment only) from April to September. The multisport area is ideal for football, basketball, tennis, table tennis, badminton and beach volleyball, and there is also a skateboard ramp.

☐ Multilingual children's club – pre-school
☑ Multilingual children's club – 5-10 year olds
☑ Multilingual children's club – 10-14 year olds
☑ Creative crafts
☑ Bicycle hire for children
☑ Facilities for children in wash blocks
☑ Children's pool
☑ Children's play area
☐ Crèche and/or babysitting
☑ Local information of interest for children

Camp du Domaine

B.P. 207 La Favière, F-83230 Bormes-les-Mimosas (Var)
t: 04 94 71 03 12 e: mail@campdudomaine.com
alanrogers.com/FR83120 www.campdudomaine.com

Accommodation: ☑Pitch ☑Mobile home/chalet ☐ Hotel/B&B ☐ Apartment

Camp du Domaine, 3 km. south of Le Lavandou, is a large, attractive beachside site with 1,200 pitches set in 45 hectares of pinewood, although surprisingly it does not give the impression of being so big. The pitches are large (up to 200 sq.m) and most are reasonably level, 800 with 10A electricity. The most popular pitches are beside the beach, but the ones furthest away are generally larger and have more shade. Amongst the trees, many are more suitable for tents. The price for all the pitches is the same – smaller but near the beach or larger with shade. The beach is the attraction and everyone tries to get close. American motorhomes are not accepted. Despite its size, the site does not feel too busy, except perhaps around the supermarket. This is mainly because many pitches are hidden in the trees, the access roads are quite wide and it all covers quite a large area (some of the beach pitches are 600 m. from the entrance). Its popularity makes early reservation necessary over a long season.

Special offers

Special offer on bungalow and mobile home rental for five people: the second week is half price, with the lowest prices in May and June.

You might like to know

Adventurous campers can try their hand at parasailing, only a short distance from the site. There are plenty of water-based activities to choose from including windsurfing and deep-sea fishing.

☐ Multilingual children's club – pre-school
☑ Multilingual children's club – 5-10 year olds
☑ Multilingual children's club – 10-14 year olds
☑ Creative crafts
☐ Bicycle hire for children
☑ Facilities for children in wash blocks
☐ Children's pool
☑ Children's play area
☐ Crèche and/or babysitting
☑ Local information of interest for children

Facilities: Ten modern, well used but clean toilet blocks. Mostly Turkish WCs. Facilities for disabled visitors (but steep steps). Baby room. Washing machines. Fridge hire. Well stocked supermarket, bars, pizzeria (all open all season). No swimming pool. Excellent play area. Boats, pedaloes for hire. Wide range of watersports. Games, competitions (July/Aug). Children's club. Tennis. Multisport courts. Barbecues are strictly forbidden. Dogs are not accepted 10/7-21/8. Off site: Bicycle hire 500 m. Riding and golf 15 km.

Open: 9 April - 5 November.

Directions: From Bormes-les Mimosas, head east on D559 to Le Lavandou. At roundabout, turn off D559 towards the sea on road signed Favière. After 2 km. turn left at site signs. GPS: 43.11779, 6.35176

Charges guide

Per unit incl. 2 persons and electricity	€ 27,00 - € 39,00
extra person	€ 5,60 - € 8,50
child (under 7 yrs)	free - € 4,50

Domaine Naturiste de Bélézy

F-84410 Bédoin (Vaucluse)
t: 04 90 65 60 18 e: info@belezy.com
alanrogers.com/FR84020 www.belezy.com

Accommodation: ☑Pitch ☑Mobile home/chalet ☐ Hotel/B&B ☐ Apartment

At the foot of Mt Ventoux, surrounded by beautiful scenery, Bélézy is an excellent naturist site with many amenities and activities and the ambience is relaxed and comfortable. The 320 pitches, 248 for touring (12A electricity, long leads required) are set amongst many varieties of trees and shrubs giving space and privacy. The attractive bar/restaurant and terrace overlook the swimming pool area and have superb views over the large recreational area and hills beyond. The site has an ecological theme with a small farm, fishpond and a vegetable garden especially for the children. Near the pool area is a smart restaurant, with terrace, and the mellow old Mas (Provençal farmhouse) that houses many of the activities and amenities. There is a hydrotherapy centre to tone up and revitalise, with qualified diagnosis, Chinese medicine (including acupuncture) and Bach therapies. Activities are arranged including painting, pottery courses and language lessons (not July/Aug) and music (bring your own instrument).

Special offers
Children under eight go free between 30/6 and 6/7, and between 27/8 and 5/10.

You might like to know
An educational farm runs during summer with animals and an organic kitchen garden (the children's cookery lessons use the home-grown produce).

- ☑ Multilingual children's club – pre-school
- ☑ Multilingual children's club – 5-10 year olds
- ☑ Multilingual children's club – 10-14 year olds
- ☑ Creative crafts
- ☑ Bicycle hire for children
- ☑ Facilities for children in wash blocks
- ☑ Children's pool
- ☑ Children's play area
- ☑ Crèche and/or babysitting
- ☑ Local information of interest for children

Facilities: Four toilet blocks with very good facilities for campers with disabilities – newer ones are excellent, some have hot showers in the open air. A superb children's section. Shop (2/4-25/9). Excellent restaurant/takeaway (2/4-25/9). Swimming pools. Sauna. Tennis. Adventure play area. Activities all season. Archery. Guided walks. Children's club. Hydrotherapy centre (2/4-25/9). Pets are not accepted. Charcoal barbecues are not permitted. Off site: Bédoin with shops and restaurants 1.5 km. Discover the riches of Provence with its many interesting old market towns and villages. Superb area for walking and cycling with the challenge of Mont Ventoux.

Open: 23 March - 2 October.

Directions: From A7 autoroute (exit 22) or the RN7, south of Orange, take D950 southeast to Carpentras, then D974 northeast to Bédoin. In Bédoin turn right at roundabout, site signed, site is 2 km. GPS: 44.13352, 5.18745

Charges guide

Per unit incl. 2 persons and electricity	€ 22,00 - € 39,00
extra person	€ 6,00 - € 9,40
child (3-8 yrs)	free - € 9,30

Camping Les Genêts

Avenue des Épines, F-85160 Saint Jean-de-Monts (Vendée)
t: 02 51 58 93 94   e: info@sunmarina.com
alanrogers.com/FR85006   www.sunmarina.com

Accommodation: ☑ Pitch ☑ Mobile home/chalet   ☐ Hotel/B&B ☐ Apartment

Les Genêts is an excellent choice for a seaside holiday. The site can be found 800 m. from a fine sandy beach to the south of the popular resort of St Jean-de-Monts, and is surrounded by pine forest and dunes. It is one of four sites owned by the Sunmarina group. Pitches are large, well shaded and are all divided by bushes and shrubs. A range of fully equipped mobile homes and chalets are available to rent. There is an excellent aqua park with multi-track water slides. This is a lively site in high season (July/August) with plenty of activities for all ages. The nearest beach is at les Marines and there are several shops and restaurants adjacent. St Jean, to the north, is an important resort with all facilities, including miles of excellent cycle tracks. The town's entire seafront has benefited immeasurably from a five year restoration programme and it is a delightful place for an evening stroll.

You might like to know

Ask at reception to book your first scuba dive in the swimming pool – a great opportunity to try this wonderful sport.

☑ Multi-lingual children's club – pre-school
☑ Multi-lingual children's club – 5-10 year olds
☑ Multi-lingual children's club – 10-14 year olds
☐ Creative crafts
☐ Bicycle hire for children
☑ Facilities for children in wash blocks
☑ Children's pool
☑ Children's play area
☐ Crèche and/or babysitting
☑ Local information of interest for children

Facilities: Good sanitary blocks with hot showers, baby room and children toilets. Laundry facilities. Covered swimming pool, jacuzzi and outdoor slides. Restaurant. Shop. Bar. Internet access available. Entertainment in high season. Off site: Golf 6 km. Riding 2 km. Canoeing. Fishing port. Cliffs. The Rocky Côte Sauvage and Puy du Fou. Beach at St Jean-de-Monts.

Open: 10 May - 15 September.

Directions: Follow the coastal road of St Jean-de-Monts, D38 south towards les Sables d'Olonne. GPS: 46.754093, -2.012815

Charges guide

Per unit incl. 2 persons and electricity	€ 25,00 - € 34,00

Camping la Yole

Chemin des Bosses, Orouet, F-85160 Saint Jean-de-Monts (Vendée)
t: 02 51 58 67 17   e: contact@la-yole.com
alanrogers.com/FR85150   www.la-yole.com

Accommodation: ☑ Pitch ☑ Mobile home/chalet   ☐ Hotel/B&B ☐ Apartment

La Yole is an attractive and well run site, two kilometres from a sandy beach. It offers 369 pitches, some of which are occupied by tour operators and mobile homes to rent. There are 180 touring pitches, most with shade and separated by bushes and trees. A newer area at the rear of the site is a little more open. All the pitches are of at least 100 sq.m. and have electricity (10A), water and drainage. The pool complex includes an attractive outdoor pool, a paddling pool, slide and an indoor heated pool with jacuzzi. There are also new gym facilities. Entertainment is organised in high season. This is a clean and tidy site, ideal for families with children and you will receive a helpful and friendly welcome.

You might like to know

Camping la Yole is perfect for families with children under 13, who will love the enormous playground and happy atmosphere where they can make lots of new friends.

☐ Multilingual children's club – pre-school
☑ Multilingual children's club – 5-10 year olds
☐ Multilingual children's club – 10-14 year olds
☑ Creative crafts
☑ Bicycle hire for children
☑ Facilities for children in wash blocks
☑ Children's pool
☑ Children's play area
☐ Crèche and/or babysitting
☐ Local information of interest for children

Facilities: Two toilet blocks include washbasins in cabins and facilities for disabled visitors and babies. A third block has a baby room. Laundry facilities. Shop (15/5-5/9). Bar, restaurant and takeaway (1/5-15/9). Outdoor pool and paddling pool. Indoor heated pool with jacuzzi (all season, no shorts). Gym centre. Play area. Club room. Tennis. Games room. Entertainment in high season. WiFi (charged). Gas barbecues only. Max. 1 dog. Off site: Beach, bus service, bicycle hire 2 km. Riding 3 km. Fishing, golf and watersports 6 km.

Open: 2 April - 21 September.

Directions: Site is signed off the D38, 6 km. south of St Jean-de-Monts in the village of Orouet. Coming from St Jean-de-Monts turn right at l'Oasis restaurant towards Mouette and follow signs to site. GPS: 46.75659, -2.00792

Charges guide

Per unit incl. 2 persons	
and electricity	€ 16,00 - € 31,00
extra person	€ 3,70 - € 6,80
child (under 9 yrs)	free - € 5,50
dog	€ 4,00 - € 5,00

Kawan Village Lac de Bouzey

19 rue du Lac, F-88390 Sanchey (Vosges)
t: **03 29 82 49 41** e: **lacdebouzey@orange.fr**
alanrogers.com/FR88040 www.lacdebouzey.com

Accommodation: ☑ Pitch ☑ Mobile home/chalet ☐ Hotel/B&B ☐ Apartment

Open all year, Camping Lac de Bouzey is 8 km. west of Épinal, at the start of the Vosges Massif. The 147 reasonably level grass pitches are separated by very tall trees and some hedging giving varying amounts of shade. There are 107 for touring, all with electricity (6/10A) and 100 are fully serviced. They are on a gently sloping hillside above the lake and there are views over the lake and its sandy beaches. In high season there is entertainment for all ages, especially teenagers, and the site will be very lively. Many watersports may be enjoyed, from pedaloes to canoes, windsurfing and sailing. The large, imposing building at the entrance to the site houses a restaurant and bar with terraces overlooking the lake, and the underground disco. Two bars by the lake would indicate that the lakeside is popular with the public in summer but the camping area is quiet, separated by a road and well back and above the main entrance. It is well placed for exploring the hills, valleys, lakes and waterfalls of the south of Alsace Lorraine.

You might like to know
The poolside shows, two evenings a week, are a popular social event for people of all ages.

- ☑ Multilingual children's club – pre-school
- ☑ Multilingual children's club – 5-10 year olds
- ☑ Multilingual children's club – 10-14 year olds
- ☑ Creative crafts
- ☑ Bicycle hire for children
- ☑ Facilities for children in wash blocks
- ☑ Children's pool
- ☑ Children's play area
- ☐ Crèche and/or babysitting
- ☑ Local information of interest for children

Facilities: The refurbished toilet block includes a baby room and one for disabled visitors (there are some gradients). Small, heated section in the main building with toilet, washbasin and shower is used in winter. Laundry facilities. Motorcaravan service point. Shop and bar (all year), restaurant and takeaway (1/3-1/11). Heated pool (1/5-30/9). Fishing. Riding. Games room. Archery. Bicycle hire. Internet access. Soundproofed room for cinema shows and discos (high season). Lake beach, bathing and boating. WiFi. Off site: Golf 8 km.

Open: All year.

Directions: Site is 8 km. west of Épinal on the D460. From Épinal follow signs for Lac de Bouzey and Sanchey. At western end of Sanchey turn south, site signed. GPS: 48.16692, 6.35990

Charges guide

Per unit incl. 2 persons and electricity	€ 23,00 - € 34,00
extra person	€ 6,00 - € 10,00
child (4-10 yrs)	free - € 7,00
dog	free - € 4,00

Trevornick Holiday Park

Holywell Bay, Newquay TR8 5PW (Cornwall)
t: **01637 830531** e: **bookings@trevornick.co.uk**
alanrogers.com/UK0220 www.trevornick.co.uk

Accommodation: ☑Pitch ☐ Mobile home/chalet ☐ Hotel/B&B ☐ Apartment

Trevornick, once a working farm, is a modern, busy and well run family touring park providing a very wide range of amenities close to one of Cornwall's finest beaches. A modern reception with welcoming staff sets the tone for your holiday. The park is well managed with facilities and standards constantly monitored. It has grown to provide caravanners and campers with some 550 large grass pitches (350 with 10A electricity and 55 fully serviced with electricity, water, drainage and TV connection with DVD channel) on five level fields and two terraced areas. There are few trees but some good views. Providing 'all singing, all dancing' facilities for fun packed family holidays, the Farm Club provides varied entertainment. The sandy beach is five minutes by car or a downhill walk from the park. An innovative idea is the Hire Shop where it is possible rent anything you might have forgotten, from sheets, a fridge, a travel cot, to a camera or a wet suit to catch the famous Cornish surf!

You might like to know

There is a brilliant sandy beach nearby.

- ☑ Multilingual children's club – pre-school
- ☑ Multilingual children's club – 5-10 year olds
- ☑ Multilingual children's club – 10-14 year olds
- ☑ Creative crafts
- ☑ Bicycle hire for children
- ☑ Facilities for children in wash blocks
- ☑ Children's pool
- ☑ Children's play area
- ☐ Crèche and/or babysitting
- ☑ Local information of interest for children

Facilities: Five modern toilet blocks provide showers, two family bathrooms, baby bath, laundry facilities and provision for disabled visitors. Well stocked supermarket (from late May). Hire Shop. Bars (with TV), restaurant, café and takeaway. Entertainment (every night in season). Pool complex with heated outdoor pool, paddling pool, sunbathing decks, solarium, sauna and massage chair. Health and beauty salon. Super Fort Knox style adventure playground. Arcade and bowling alley. Teenagers' room. 18-hole pitch-and-putt with golf pro shop. Bicycle hire. Coarse fishing with three lakes. Only limited facilities open at Easter and from 8 Sept. Off site: Riding within 2 miles. Bicycle hire and boat launching 4 miles.

Open: Easter; mid May - mid September.

Directions: From A3075 approach to the Newquay - Perranporth road, turn towards Cubert and Holywell Bay. Continue through Cubert to park on the right.
GPS: 50.384983, -5.128933

Charges guide

Per person	£ 5,45 - £ 10,20
child (3-14 yrs)	£ 1,45 - £ 7,20
electricity	£ 5,15 - £ 5,65
dog	£ 4,10 - £ 5,10

Stowford Farm Meadows

Berry Down, Combe Martin, Ilfracombe EX34 0PW (Devon)
t: **01271 882476**   e: **enquiries@stowford.co.uk**
alanrogers.com/UK0690   www.stowford.co.uk

Accommodation: ☑Pitch ☐ Mobile home/chalet ☐ Hotel/B&B ☐ Apartment

Stowford Farm is a friendly, family park set in 500 acres of the rolling North Devon countryside, available for recreation and walking, yet within easy reach of five local beaches. The touring park and its facilities have been developed in the fields and farm buildings surrounding the attractive old farmhouse and provide a village like centre with a comfortable spacious feel. There are 710 pitches on five slightly sloping meadows separated by Devon hedges of beech and ash. Stowford also provides plenty to keep the whole family occupied without leaving the park, including woodland walks and horse riding from the park's own stables. The Old Stable Bar offers entertainment in high season including barn dances, discos, karaoke and other musical evenings. There is also much for children to do, from the indoor heated pool and covered mini zoo (Petorama) where they can handle many sorts of animals (on payment), to the wide range of organised activities on offer.

You might like to know

This is a peaceful site, with plenty to do for children and some great views from the lovely heated pool.

- ☑ Multilingual children's club – pre-school
- ☑ Multilingual children's club – 5-10 year olds
- ☑ Multilingual children's club – 10-14 year olds
- ☑ Creative crafts
- ☐ Bicycle hire for children
- ☑ Facilities for children in wash blocks
- ☑ Children's pool
- ☑ Children's play area
- ☐ Crèche and/or babysitting
- ☑ Local information of interest for children

Facilities: Five identical toilet blocks, each looked after by resident wardens, are fully equipped and provide good, functional facilities, each block with laundry facilities and dishwashing. The newest block (in field 5) has under-floor heating and includes facilities for disabled visitors. Well stocked shop (with holiday goods and gas). Good value takeaway with restaurant area. Bars and entertainment in season. Indoor pool (22x10 m; heated Easter-Oct) at a small charge. Riding. 18-hole pitch and putt. Crazy golf. 'Kiddies kar' track (all charged). Games room. Large play area. Games and activities organised in high season. WiFi. ATM. Woodland walks. Off site: Fishing and boat launching 4 miles. Bicycle hire 10 miles.

Open: All year.

Directions: From Barnstaple take A39 towards Lynton. After 1 mile turn left on B3230. Turn right at garage on A3123 and park is 1.5 miles on the right. GPS: 51.174983, -4.05475

Charges guide

Per unit incl. 2 persons and electricity	£ 10,40 - £ 23,00
extra person	free - £ 4,50
child (5-12 yrs)	free - £ 4,50
dog	£ 1,60 - £ 2,60

Woolacombe Sands Holiday Park

Beach Road, Woolacombe EX34 7AF (Devon)
t: 01271 870569 e: lifesabeach@woolacombe-sands.co.uk
alanrogers.com/UK0735 www.woolacombe-sands.co.uk

Accommodation: ☑Pitch ☑Mobile home/chalet ☐ Hotel/B&B ☐ Apartment

With sea views and within walking distance of Woolacombe's lovely sandy beach, this family park has been terraced out of the valley side as you drop down into the village. Apart from its smart entrance, it has been left natural. The pond and stream at the bottom are almost hidden with gated access to the National Trust fields across the valley. The 200 terraced level grass pitches, all with 16A electricity, are accessed by gravel roads with some good up-and-down walking needed to the toilet blocks. Some 50 mobile homes and 14 bungalows are in the more central area, and tents tend to be placed on the bottom terraces. The park boasts both indoor and outdoor pools with a full time attendant. Upstairs from the indoor pool is a very pleasant conservatory seating area with great views and an outside seating area adjacent to it. Evenings see Woolly Bear emerge from his 'shack' to entertain children, with adult entertainment later. A useful path leads from the site to the beach and the walk is said to take 15 minutes.

You might like to know

A wide range of enjoyable day trips are possible from Woolacombe Sands, including boat trips along the north Devon coast.

☐ Multilingual children's club – pre-school
☑ Multilingual children's club – 5-10 year olds
☐ Multilingual children's club – 10-14 year olds
☑ Creative crafts
☐ Bicycle hire for children
☑ Facilities for children in wash blocks
☑ Children's pool
☑ Children's play area
☐ Crèche and/or babysitting
☑ Local information of interest for children

Facilities: Four basic toilet blocks with hot water are spread amongst the terraces. The newer shower block has separate toilets opposite. Shop. Self-service food bar providing good value meals and breakfast (main season and B.Hs). Two bars and full entertainment programme. Heated indoor and outdoor pools both with paddling pool areas. Fenced play area on bark. Ball area with nets. Crazy golf. Kingpin bowling. Off site: Riding next door. Golf, bicycle hire and freshwater fishing 0.5 miles. Beach 15 minutes walk or 0.5 miles.

Open: 1 April - 30 October.

Directions: Follow A361 from Barnstaple through Braunton towards Ilfracombe. At Mullacott Cross roundabout turn left for Woolacombe (B3343). Site clearly signed on left as you go down the hill into the village. GPS: 51.17145, -4.191833

Charges guide

Per person (incl. electricity)	£ 5,00 - £ 15,00
child (4-15 yrs)	£ 2,50 - £ 7,50
dog	£ 5,00

Beverley Park

Goodrington Road, Paignton TQ4 7JE (Devon)
t: **01803 661978** e: **info@beverley-holidays.co.uk**
alanrogers.com/UK0870 www.beverley-holidays.co.uk

Accommodation: ☑Pitch ☑Mobile home/chalet ☐ Hotel/B&B ☐ Apartment

Beverley Park is an amazing holiday centre catering for every need. It has been developed and run by the Jeavons family for over 50 years to very high standards. It is popular, busy and attractively landscaped with marvellous views over Torbay. The pools, a large dance hall, bars and entertainment, are all run in an efficient and orderly manner. The park has 190 caravan holiday homes and 23 lodges, mainly around the central complex. There are 179 touring pitches in the lower areas of the park, all reasonably sheltered, some with views across the bay and some on slightly sloping ground. All pitches can take awnings and 87 have 16A electricity, 38 have hardstanding and 42 are fully serviced. Tents are accepted. Entertainment is organised at Easter and from early May in the Starlight Cabaret bar. There are indoor and outdoor pools, each one heated and supervised. This popular park has lots to offer and is well maintained and run. A member of the Best of British group.

You might like to know

Why not visit the picturesque harbour at Brixham or the beautiful and tranquil Buckfast Abbey?

☐ Multilingual children's club – pre-school
☑ Multilingual children's club – 5-10 year olds
☑ Multilingual children's club – 10-14 year olds
☑ Creative crafts
☐ Bicycle hire for children
☑ Facilities for children in wash blocks
☑ Children's pool
☑ Children's play area
☐ Crèche and/or babysitting
☑ Local information of interest for children

Facilities: Good toilet blocks adjacent to the pitches, well maintained and heated, include roomy showers, some with washbasins en-suite. Baths on payment. Unit for disabled visitors. Facilities for babies. Laundry. Gas supplies. Motorcaravan service point. Large general shop (29/3-29/10). Restaurant, bars and takeaway (all Easter, then 30/4-29/10, and Autumn half-term). Heated swimming pools, outdoor 28/5-4/9, indoor all year. Fitness centre. Tennis. Crazy golf. Playground. Nature trail. Amusement centre. Soft play area. Dogs are not accepted.
Off site: Regular minibus service to Paignton (timetable at reception) or public services from outside the park. Fishing, bicycle hire, riding and golf all within 2 miles.

Open: All year.

Directions: Park is south of Paignton in Goodrington Road between A379 coast road and B3203 ring road and is well signed on both. GPS: 50.413533, -3.568667

Charges guide

Per unit incl. 2 persons and electricity	£ 15,10 - £ 32,30
tent pitch incl. 2 persons	£ 12,60 - £ 28,20
extra person	£ 4,70
child	£ 3,50

Woodlands Grove

Blackawton, Dartmouth TQ9 7DQ (Devon)
t: **01803 712598** e: **holiday@woodlandsgrove.com**
alanrogers.com/UK0840 www.woodlands-caravanpark.com

Accommodation: ☑Pitch ☐ Mobile home/chalet ☐ Hotel/B&B ☐ Apartment

Woodlands is a pleasant surprise – from the road you have no idea of just what is hidden away deep in the Devon countryside. To achieve this, there has been sympathetic development of farm and woodland to provide a leisure centre, which is open to the public and offers a range of activities and entertainment appealing to all ages. The camping and caravan site overlooks the woodland and the leisure park, taking 350 units on three sloping, grassy fields. Children (and many energetic parents too!) will thoroughly enjoy a huge variety of imaginative adventure play equipment, amazing water coasters, toboggan runs, the 'Sea Dragon Swing Ship', a white knuckle monster, the 'Avalanche' and much more, hidden amongst the trees. The 'Empire of the Sea Dragon', an indoor play centre, provides marvellous wet weather facilities comprising five floors of play areas and amazing slides. With a two night stay, campers on the touring park are admitted free of charge to the leisure park. A member of the Best of British group.

Special offers
For stays of 2 nights or more, families receive free entry to the adjoining Woodlands Family Theme Park (16 family rides, 11 playzones, zoo-farm and vast covered play areas) – fun guaranteed, whatever the weather!

You might like to know
Woodlands Grove, an England 5-star site and a member of the Best of British group, has won the AA Campsite of the Year award, and is a previous winner of Alan Rogers Best Family Campsite.

☐ Multilingual children's club – pre-school
☐ Multilingual children's club – 5-10 year olds
☐ Multilingual children's club – 10-14 year olds
☐ Creative crafts
☐ Bicycle hire for children
☑ Facilities for children in wash blocks
☑ Children's pool
☑ Children's play area
☐ Crèche and/or babysitting
☑ Local information of interest for children

Facilities: Three modern, heated toilet blocks, include private bathrooms (coin-operated, 20p) and 16 family shower cubicles. Two laundry rooms. Freezer for ice packs. Baby facilities. The leisure park café provides good value meals and a takeaway service for campers. Café opening hours and camping shop (with gas and basic food supplies) vary according to season and demand. TV and games room. Dogs are accepted on the campsite but not in the leisure park (kennels available). Caravan storage. Off site: Golf 0.5 miles. Riding 5 miles. Beach and fishing 4 miles. The charming town of Dartmouth and the South Hams beaches.

Open: Easter - 1 November.

Directions: From A38 at Buckfastleigh, take A384 to Totnes. Before the town centre turn right on A381 Kingsbridge road. After Halwell turn left at Totnes Cross, on A3122 to Dartmouth. Park is 2.5 miles. GPS: 50.357898, -3.675001

Charges guide

Per unit incl. 2 persons and electricity	£ 16,50 - £ 26,50
extra person over 2 yrs	£ 7,75
awning or extra small pup tent	£ 3,50
dog (contact site first)	£ 2,75

Wareham Forest Tourist Park

North Trigon, Wareham BH20 7NZ (Dorset)
t: **01929 551393** e: **holiday@warehamforest.co.uk**
alanrogers.com/UK2030 www.warehamforest.co.uk

Accommodation: ☑Pitch ☑Mobile home/chalet ☐ Hotel/B&B ☐ Apartment

This peacefully located and spacious park, on the edge of Wareham Forest, has 200 pitches and is continually being upgraded by its enthusiastic owners, Tony and Sarah Birch. The focal point of the park is the modern reception and shop, located by the pools. Four main areas provide a wide choice of touring pitches from grass to hardstanding and luxury, all with 16A electricity. Tenters have their own choice of open field or pinewood. The site has provided direct access for walkers into the forest or the seven miles of the Sika cycle trail may be used. The lovely market town of Wareham is accessible by bike without having to use the roads. This park has an almost continental feel, with plenty of space. Even when it is busy, it is calm and peaceful in its forest setting. In low season you may be lucky enough to spot the herd of Sika deer which live in the forest. The park is well situated to explore the Dorset coast and Thomas Hardy country. A member of the Best of British Group.

You might like to know

Why not go to Monkey World or the Dinosaur Museum? Both are just 30 minutes away.

☐ Multilingual children's club – pre-school
☐ Multilingual children's club – 5-10 year olds
☐ Multilingual children's club – 10-14 year olds
☐ Creative crafts
☑ Bicycle hire for children
☐ Facilities for children in wash blocks
☑ Children's pool
☑ Children's play area
☐ Crèche and/or babysitting
☐ Local information of interest for children

Facilities: Two well maintained toilet blocks are of a good standard with some washbasins in cubicles. Main block recently completely refurbished and both blocks are centrally heated. Facilities for disabled visitors. Well equipped laundry rooms. Motorcaravan service point. Small licensed shop with gas. Swimming pool (60x20 ft), heated 20/5-15/9. Large adventure play area. Barrier closed 23.00-07.00. Resident wardens on site. Caravan storage. WiFi. Off site: Cycle trail and walking in the forest. Bicycle hire and golf 3 miles. Fishing 5 miles. Riding 8 miles.

Open: All year.

Directions: From A31 Bere Regis, follow the A35 towards Poole for 0.5 miles and turn right where signed to Wareham. Drive for 1.5 miles. First park on the left as you enter the forest. GPS: 50.721733, -2.156217

Charges guide

Per unit incl. 2 persons and electricity	£ 16,00 - £ 34,00
'superior' pitch fully serviced	£ 18,75 - £ 37,50
extra person	£ 3,00 - £ 5,50
child (5-15 yrs)	£ 2,00 - £ 3,90
dog	free - £ 1,50

Sandy Balls Holiday Centre

Godshill, Fordingbridge SP6 2JZ (Hampshire)
t: 0845 270 2248 e: post@sandy-balls.co.uk
alanrogers.com/UK2290 www.sandy-balls.co.uk

Accommodation: ☑ Pitch ☑ Mobile home/chalet ☐ Hotel/B&B ☐ Apartment

Sandy Balls sits high above the sweep of the Avon river near Fordingbridge, amidst woodland which is protected as a nature reserve. Very well run and open all year, the 120 acre park has many private holiday homes as well as 26 caravan holiday homes and 117 lodges for rent. The touring areas have 233 marked, hedged, serviced pitches for caravans and tents on part-hardstanding and part-grass, with 16A electricity and TV connections. In August there is an additional unmarked tent area. A woodland leisure trail allows wild animals and birds to be observed in their natural surroundings and the attractions of the New Forest are close at hand. The heart of this holiday centre is the architecturally designed, multi-million pound 'village'. With its traffic-free piazza, here are the bistro, pub, Guest Services bureau, gift shop, cycle shop, small supermarket and leisure club, all designed to blend in with the forest surroundings and provide space to relax and meet friends. A member of the Best of British Group.

You might like to know

Don't forget to take your bike – it's a fun way to explore the New Forest national park.

☐ Multilingual children's club – pre-school
☑ Multilingual children's club – 5-10 year olds
☑ Multilingual children's club – 10-14 year olds
☑ Creative crafts
☑ Bicycle hire for children
☑ Facilities for children in wash blocks
☑ Children's pool
☑ Children's play area
☐ Crèche and/or babysitting
☑ Local information of interest for children

Facilities: Three refurbished toilet blocks have underfloor heating and washbasins in cubicles. One Portacabin style unit remains as an overflow in the tent field. Toilets for disabled visitors and baby facilities. Excellent central launderette. Motorcaravan service point. Entertainment (high season only). Outdoor pool (25/5-30/8). Indoor pool (66x30 ft). Well equipped gym, jacuzzi, steam room, sauna and solarium. Tempus therapy centre. Games room. Adventure playground and play areas. Soft play area. Clay modelling tuition and story telling. Tepees and tents for rent. River fishing (permit). Riding stables. Bicycle hire. Archery. Off site: Golf 6 miles. Beach 20 miles.

Open: All year.

Directions: Park is well signed 1.5 miles east of Fordingbridge on the B3078.
GPS: 50.930267, -1.7602

Charges guide

Per unit incl. 2 persons and electricity	£ 15,00 - £ 40,00
extra person	free - £ 5,00
child (0-17 yrs)	free - £ 2,00
dog	free - £ 4,00

Kelling Heath Holiday Park

Weybourne, Holt, Sheringham NR25 7HW (Norfolk)
t: **01263 588181** e: **info@kellingheath.co.uk**
alanrogers.com/UK3430 www.kellingheath.co.uk

Accommodation: ☑ Pitch ☑ Mobile home/chalet ☐ Hotel/B&B ☐ Apartment

Not many parks can boast their own railway station and Kelling Heath's own halt on the North Norfolk Steam Railway gives access to the beach at Sheringham. Set in 250 acres of woodland and heathland, this very spacious holiday park offers freedom and relaxation with 300 large, level, grass touring pitches, all with 16A electricity and six are fully serviced. Together with 384 caravan holiday homes (36 to let, the rest privately owned), they blend easily into the part-wooded, part-open heath. A wide range of facilities provides activities for all ages. 'The Forge' has an entertainment bar and a family room, with comprehensive entertainment all season. The leisure centre provides an indoor pool, spa pool, sauna, steam rooms and gym. An adventure playground with assault course is near. The park's natural environment allows for woodland walks, a nature trail and cycling trails, and a small lake for fishing (permit holders only). Other amenities include two hard tennis courts and a small, outdoor heated fun pool.

You might like to know

The Kelling Heath Holiday Park has its own Countryside Team to take care of the environment and share their expertise with customers.

☐ Multilingual children's club – pre-school
☑ Multilingual children's club – 5-10 year olds
☑ Multilingual children's club – 10-14 year olds
☐ Creative crafts
☐ Bicycle hire for children
☑ Facilities for children in wash blocks
☑ Children's pool
☑ Children's play area
☐ Crèche and/or babysitting
☐ Local information of interest for children

Facilities: Three toilet blocks include facilities for disabled visitors, a baby room and dishwashing and laundry sinks. Laundry facilities. Well stocked shop. Gas. Bar, restaurant and takeaway (all season). Indoor leisure centre with pool, gym, etc. with trained staff (membership on either daily or weekly basis). Outdoor pool (main season). Adventure play area. Tennis. Fishing. Bicycle hire. Entertainment programme. Special environmental Acorn activities for the family. WiFi (charged). Torches useful. Off site: The Norfolk coast, Felbrigg Hall, the Walsingham Shrine and the Norfolk Broads National Park are nearby. Many bird and nature reserves.

Open: 10 February - 2 January.

Directions: On A148 road from Holt to Cromer, after High Kelling, turn left just before Bodham village (international sign) signed Weybourne. Follow road for about 1 mile to park.
GPS: 52.92847, 1.13663

Charges guide

Per unit incl. electricity	£ 18,00 - £ 32,30
with full services	£ 23,45 - £ 39,00
dog (max. 2)	£ 3,10 - £ 5,15
awning	£ 2,10 - £ 5,15

Skipsea Sands Holiday Park

Mill Lane, Skipsea YO25 8TZ (East Yorkshire)
t: 0871 664 9812 e: skipsea.sands@parkresorts.com
alanrogers.com/UK4496 www.park-resortstouring.com/skipseasands

Accommodation: ☑Pitch ☑Mobile home/chalet ☐ Hotel/B&B ☐ Apartment

This well established holiday park is now owned by Park Resorts and is primarily dedicated to caravan holiday homes, of which there are 625 privately owned and 70 to rent. There is however a pleasantly laid out touring park occupying its own corner of the site and bordered by an attractive duck pond and a large playing area (both well fenced). The 91 marked, level pitches (some occupied by seasonal caravans) are separated by hedges and all have electricity (16A); some also have water, drainage and sewerage connections. The leisure facilities are outstanding and a full daily programme of activities and entertainment is offered for children and adults. Situated on the cliffs on the Yorkshire coast south of Bridlington, beaches are either a good walk or a short drive away. There is a wide choice of possible days out: Beverley or York, each with its Minster and its horse racing; Spurn Point or Bempton Cliffs (RSPB); Cruckley Animal Farm or Bondville Miniature Village.

You might like to know

Why not try a completely new activity such as the hydrodrome, jet racers or maybe some raft building?

☑ Multilingual children's club – pre-school
☑ Multilingual children's club – 5-10 year olds
☑ Multilingual children's club – 10-14 year olds
☑ Creative crafts
☐ Bicycle hire for children
☐ Facilities for children in wash blocks
☐ Children's pool
☑ Children's play area
☐ Crèche and/or babysitting
☑ Local information of interest for children

Facilities: Two heated toilet blocks have been refurbished, with pushbutton showers, open washbasins and en-suite facilities for disabled visitors. Motorcaravan service point. Washing machines and dryers. Well stocked shop. Bar, coffee shop and restaurant with takeaway. Leisure centre with sports hall, ten-pin bowling, heated indoor pool, jacuzzi, sauna and steam room. Fitness centre with gym and sunbed. Games 'Kingdom' with electronic games and 'Kids' Zone'. WiFi (charged). Off site: Buses from park gates. Village with shops, pub, restaurant 1 mile. Beach 0.25 mile (on foot) or 4 miles (by car). Golf 3 miles. Boat launching 6 miles.

Open: 1 March - 31 October.

Directions: Skipsea is 20 miles northeast of Hull and 10 miles south of Bridlington. From the Humber Bridge or from the M62, take A63 to Hull, east of city follow signs to join the A165 towards Bridlington. After 18 miles, turn east on B1249 to Skipsea. In village, turn right then left to site (signed). GPS: 53.98957, -0.20716

Charges guide

Per unit incl. all services	£ 6,00 - £ 30,00
tent pitch	£ 5,00 - £ 25,00
dog	£ 1,00 - £ 3,00

Brighouse Bay Holiday Park

Brighouse Bay, Borgue, Kirkcudbright DG6 4TS (Dumfries and Galloway)

t: **01557 870267**   e: **info@gillespie-leisure.co.uk**

alanrogers.com/UK6950   **www.brighouse-bay.co.uk**

Accommodation: ☑Pitch ☑Mobile home/chalet ☐ Hotel/B&B ☐ Apartment

Hidden away within 1,200 exclusive acres, on a quiet, unspoilt peninsula, this spacious family park is only some 200 yards through bluebell woods from a lovely sheltered bay. It has exceptional all weather facilities, as well as golf and pony trekking. Most of the 210 touring pitches have electricity (10/16A), some with hardstanding and some with water, drainage and TV aerial. Three tent areas are on fairly flat, undulating ground and some pitches have electricity. There are 120 self-contained holiday caravans and lodges of which about 30 are let, the rest privately owned. On site leisure facilities include a golf and leisure club with 16.5 m. pool, water features, jacuzzi, steam room, fitness room, games room (all on payment), golf driving range, bowling green and clubhouse bar and bistro. Like the park, these facilities are open all year. The Pony Trekking Centre, also open all year, offers treks for complete beginners and hacks for the more experienced. This is a well run park with high standards. A member of the Best of British Group.

You might like to know

Brighouse Bay has been developed along very eco-friendly principles, and is now one of the most environmentally sustainable campsites in the UK.

☐ Multilingual children's club – pre-school
☐ Multilingual children's club – 5-10 year olds
☐ Multilingual children's club – 10-14 year olds
☐ Creative crafts
☑ Bicycle hire for children
☑ Facilities for children in wash blocks
☐ Children's pool
☑ Children's play area
☐ Crèche and/or babysitting
☑ Local information of interest for children

Facilities: The large, well maintained main toilet block includes 10 unisex cabins with shower, basin and WC, and 12 with washbasin and WC. A second, excellent block next to the tent areas has en-suite shower rooms (one for disabled visitors) and bathroom and baby room. One section is heated in winter. Laundry facilities. Motorcaravan service point. Gas supplies. Licensed supermarket. Bar, restaurant and takeaway (all year). Golf and Leisure Club with indoor pool (all year). Play area (incl. new one for under 5s). Riding centre. Mountain bike hire. Quad bikes, boating pond, 10-pin bowling, playgrounds, putting. Nature trails. Coarse fishing ponds plus sea angling and an all-tide slipway.

Open: All year.

Directions: In Kirkcudbright turn onto A755 and cross river bridge. In 400 yds. turn left onto the B727 at international camping sign. Or follow Brighouse Bay signs off A75 just east of Gatehouse of Fleet. GPS: 54.7875, -4.1291

Charges guide

Per unit incl. 2 persons and electricity	£ 19,70 - £ 26,00
extra person	£ 2,65
child (4-15 yrs)	£ 1,80
dog	£ 2,50

Camping Birkelt

1 Um Birkelt, L-7633 Larochette
t: 879 040   e: info@camping-birkelt.lu
alanrogers.com/LU7610   www.camping-birkelt.lu

Accommodation: ☑ Pitch ☐ Mobile home/chalet ☐ Hotel/B&B ☐ Apartment

This is very much a family site, with a great range of facilities provided. It is well organised and well laid out, set in an elevated position in attractive, undulating countryside. A tarmac road runs around the site with 427 large grass pitches, some slightly sloping, many with a fair amount of shade, on either side of gravel access roads in straight rows or circles. An all weather swimming pool complex is beside the site entrance (free for campers) and entertainment for children is arranged in high season. The site is very popular with tour operators (140 pitches). The main activities take place adjacent to the large circular all-weather family pool. This is an outdoor pool in high season and covered and heated in cooler weather. Several play areas are dotted all over the site. The entrance to the site has been made vehicle-free (the vehicle entrance is on a separate road) and provides a pleasant terrace and shopping area. Throughout the site, all signage is in four languages including English.

You might like to know

Müllerthal is well known for its forests and medieval castles such as Larochette and Beaufort. A visit is highly recommended.

☑ Multilingual children's club – pre-school
☑ Multilingual children's club – 5-10 year olds
☑ Multilingual children's club – 10-14 year olds
☑ Creative crafts
☑ Bicycle hire for children
☑ Facilities for children in wash blocks
☑ Children's pool
☑ Children's play area
☐ Crèche and/or babysitting
☑ Local information of interest for children

Facilities: Three modern heated sanitary buildings well situated around the site include mostly open washbasins (6 cabins in one block). Baby baths. Facilities (including accomodation to rent) for wheelchair users. Washing machines and dryers. Motorcaravan service point. Shops. Coffee bar. Restaurant with terrace. Outdoor swimming pool (covered and heated in cooler weather). Outdoor pool for toddlers. Sauna. Play areas. Trampolines. Volleyball. Minigolf. Tennis. Bicycle hire. Riding. Balloon flights. Internet points. WiFi. Off site: Golf 5 km. Fishing and kayaking 10 km.

Open: 24 March - 4 November.

Directions: From N7 (Diekirch - Luxembourg City), turn onto N8 (CR 118) at Berschblach (just past Mersch) towards Larochette. Site is signed on the right 1.5 km. from Larochette. Approach road is fairly steep and narrow. GPS: 49.78508, 6.21033

Charges guide

Per unit incl. 2 persons and electricity	€ 19,50 - € 25,00
with water and drainage	€ 22,50 - € 38,00
extra person	€ 4,00
dog	€ 2,50

Europacamping Nommerlayen

Rue Nommerlayen, L-7465 Nommern
t: 878 078   e: nommerlayen@vo.lu
alanrogers.com/LU7620   www.nommerlayen-ec.lu

Accommodation: ☑ Pitch ☑ Mobile home/chalet ☐ Hotel/B&B ☐ Apartment

Situated at the end of its own road in the lovely wooded hills of central Luxembourg, this is a top quality site with fees to match, but it has everything! A large, central building housing most of the services and amenities opens onto a terrace around an excellent swimming pool complex with a large fun pool and an imaginative water playground. The 367 individual pitches (100 sq.m) are on grassy terraces, all have access to electricity (2/16A) and water taps. Pitches are grouped beside age-appropriate play areas and the facilities throughout the campsite reflect the attention given to families in particular. The superb new sanitary block is called Badtemple (having been built in the style of a Greek temple). Entry to the sauna and hot water for washbasins, showers and sinks is by a pre-paid smart key. Sports facilities are varied and cater for all ages. There is organised entertainment for children and families in high season, and beyond the site walking and cycle paths abound. A member of Leading Campings Group.

You might like to know
There is a 50 m. slide in the playground, and a new water playhouse for toddlers.

☐ Multilingual children's club – pre-school
☑ Multilingual children's club – 5-10 year olds
☑ Multilingual children's club – 10-14 year olds
☑ Creative crafts
☐ Bicycle hire for children
☑ Facilities for children in wash blocks
☑ Children's pool
☑ Children's play area
☐ Crèche and/or babysitting
☑ Local information of interest for children

Facilities: A large, high quality, modern sanitary unit provides some washbasins in cubicles, facilities for disabled visitors, and family and baby washrooms. The new block also includes a sauna. Twelve private bathrooms for hire. Laundry. Motorcaravan service point. Supermarket. Restaurant. Snack bar. Bar (all 4/4-8/11). Excellent swimming pool complex (1/5-15/9) and new covered and heated pool (Easter-1/11). Solarium. Fitness programmes. Bowling. Playground. Large screen TV. Entertainment in season. WiFi (charged). Off site: Riding 1 km. Fishing and golf 5 km.

Open: 1 February - 1 December.

Directions: Take the 118 road between Mersch and Larochette. Site is signed 3 km. north of Larochette towards the village of Nommern on the 346 road. GPS: 49.78472, 6.16519

Charges guide

Per unit incl. 2 persons and 2A electricity	€ 21,00 - € 38,00
extra adult	€ 5,00
child (under 18 yrs)	€ 3,50
dog	€ 2,85
electricity (16A) plus	€ 3,75

No credit cards.

Camping Kohnenhof

Kounenhaff 1, L-9838 Eisenbach
t: **929 464** e: **kohnenhof@pt.lu**
alanrogers.com/LU7680 www.campingkohnenhof.lu

Accommodation: ☑ Pitch ☑ Mobile home/chalet ☐ Hotel/B&B ☑ Apartment

Nestling in a valley with the River Our running through it, Camping Kohnenhof offers a very agreeable location for a relaxing family holiday. From the minute you stop at the reception you are assured of a warm and friendly welcome. Numerous paths cross through the wooded hillside so this could be a haven for walkers. A little bridge crosses the small river over the border to Germany. The river is shallow and safe for children (parental supervision essential). A large sports field and play area with a selection of equipment caters for younger campers. During the high season, an entertainment programme is organised for parents and children. The owner organises special golf weeks with games on different courses and discounts have been agreed at several local courses (contact the site for details). The restaurant is part of an old farmhouse and offers a wonderful ambience in which to enjoy a meal.

You might like to know

Kohnenhof is well known for its river, where customers can enjoy some relaxing fishing (permits sold at reception).

☑ Multilingual children's club – pre-school
☑ Multilingual children's club – 5-10 year olds
☑ Multilingual children's club – 10-14 year olds
☑ Creative crafts
☑ Bicycle hire for children
☐ Facilities for children in wash blocks
☑ Children's pool
☑ Children's play area
☐ Crèche and/or babysitting
☐ Local information of interest for children

Facilities: Heated sanitary block with showers and washbasins in cabins. Motorcaravan service point. Laundry. Bar, restaurant, takeaway. Games and TV room. Baker calls daily. Sports field with play equipment. Boules. Bicycle hire. Golf weeks. Discounts on six local 18-hole golf courses. WiFi. Apartments to rent. Off site: Bus to Clervaux and Vianden stops (4 times daily) outside site entrance. Riding 5 km. Castle at Vianden 14 km. Monastery at Clervaux 14 km. Golf 15 km.

Open: 15 March - 10 November.

Directions: Take N7 north from Diekirch. At Hosingen, turn right onto the narrow and winding CR324 signed Eisenbach. Follow site signs from Eisenbach or Obereisenbach.
GPS: 50.01602, 6.13600

Charges guide

Per unit incl. 2 persons and electricity	€ 19,90 - € 28,00
extra person	€ 4,00
dog	€ 3,00

Recreatiepark Klein Strand

Varsenareweg 29, B-8490 Jabbeke (West Flanders)
t: 050 811 440 e: info@kleinstrand.be
alanrogers.com/BE0555 www.kleinstrand.be

Accommodation: ☑Pitch ☑Mobile home/chalet ☐ Hotel/B&B ☐ Apartment

In a convenient location just off the A10 motorway and close to Bruges, this site is in two distinct areas divided by an access road. The touring section has 137 large pitches on flat grass separated by well-trimmed hedges; all have electricity and access to water and drainage. Though surrounded by mobile homes and seasonal caravans, this is a surprisingly relaxing area and the ambience should have been further enhanced in 2011 when a small park was created at its centre. The main site with all the privately-owned mobile homes is closer to the lake and this area has most of the amenities. These include the main reception building, restaurants, bar, minimarket, and sports facilities. This is a family holiday site and offers a comprehensive programme of activities and entertainment in July and August. The lake is used for water skiing and has a supervised swimming area with waterslides (high season) and a beach volleyball area. Klein Strand is an ideal base from which to visit Bruges (by bus) and Gent.

You might like to know

Klein Strand is within easy reach of some of Belgium's finest seaside resorts, such as Ostende, Zeebrugge and Blankenberge.

☐ Multilingual children's club – pre-school
☑ Multilingual children's club – 5-10 year olds
☑ Multilingual children's club – 10-14 year olds
☑ Creative crafts
☐ Bicycle hire for children
☑ Facilities for children in wash blocks
☑ Children's pool
☑ Children's play area
☐ Crèche and/or babysitting
☑ Local information of interest for children

Facilities: A single modern, heated, toilet block in the touring area provides the usual facilities including good sized showers (charged) and vanity style open washbasins. Baby room. Basic facilities for disabled campers. Laundry with washing machines and dryer. Dishwashing outside. Motorcaravan service point. Bar and snack bar. Children's playground. Fun pool for small children. In main park: European and Chinese restaurants, bar and snack bar, takeaways (all year). Shop (Easter-end Aug). Tennis courts and sports field. Water-ski school; water-ski shows (Sundays in July/Aug), Bicycle hire. Cable TV point (incl.) and WiFi (charged, first hour free) on all pitches. Off site: Riding 5 km. Beach 8 km. Golf and sailing 10 km.

Open: All year.

Directions: Jabbeke is 12 km. southwest of Bruges. From A18/A10 motorways, take exit 6/6B signed Jabbeke. At roundabout take first exit signed for site. In 650 m on left-hand bend, turn left to site in 600 m. Main reception is on left but in high season continue to touring site on right in 200 m. GPS: 51.18448, 3.10445

Charges guide

Per unit incl. up to 6 persons and electricity	€ 17,00 - € 34,00

NETHERLANDS – Nieuwvliet

Camping Zonneweelde

Baanstpoldersedijk 1, NL-4504 PS Nieuwvliet (Zeeland)
t: **0117 371 910**   e: **info@campingzonneweelde.nl**
alanrogers.com/NL5530   www.campingzonneweelde.nl

Accommodation: ☑ Pitch ☑ Mobile home/chalet   ☐ Hotel/B&B   ☐ Apartment

This family run site, only ten minutes walk from kilometers of wide, sandy beaches, is ideal for family holidays. In addition to pitches for 160 touring units, the site offers a wide range of chalets (20), mobile homes (200) and cabins (2), plus places for 50 seasonal caravans. Electricity connections (10A) are available throughout. Motorcaravans and twin-axle caravans are not accepted. The Natural Reserve of Het Zwin is nearby (a popular destination for birdwatching) and many interesting villages are in the area. Public transport operates in July and August from Breskens, via Sluis to visit Brugge in Belgium.

You might like to know
Special facilities for children include the aqua playground, dedicated baby changing, showers and WCs. A Dutch activity team is on site during school holidays, and there are four weeks of entertainment for teenagers during high season.

- ☑ Multilingual children's club – pre-school
- ☑ Multilingual children's club – 5-10 year olds
- ☑ Multilingual children's club – 10-14 year olds
- ☑ Creative crafts
- ☐ Bicycle hire for children
- ☑ Facilities for children in wash blocks
- ☑ Children's pool
- ☑ Children's play area
- ☐ Crèche and/or babysitting
- ☑ Local information of interest for children

Facilities: A modern, heated and well maintained sanitary building provides roomy adjustable showers and some washbasins in cabins. Children's bathroom. Also one small sanitary block with 8 WC and 4 wash cabins. Both blocks have laundry facilities. Restaurant with takeaway. Supermarket. Swimming pool (guarded in July/Aug) and separate pool for toddlers. Play areas and sports field. Bicycle hire.

Open: 3 April - 30 October.

Directions: From Westerscheldetunnel, turn right at roundabout to Breskens-Hoek-Oostburg. At Schoondijke roundabout follow signs for Breskens, Groede, turn left at first traffic lights to Groede, Nieuwvliet then right at first roundabout in Nieuwvliet. Site is signed. From Belgium: take N49 to Kaprijke and Breskens, entering NL at IJzendijke. At traffic light in Breskens turn left to Groede/Cadzand, and follow site signs. GPS: 51.382207, 3.458188

Charges guide

Per unit incl. 2 persons and electricity	€ 26,50 - € 32,00

NETHERLANDS – Wolphaartsdijk

Camping De Veerhoeve

Veerweg 48, NL-4471 NC Wolphaartsdijk (Zeeland)
t: 0113 581 155 e: info@deveerhoeve.nl
alanrogers.com/NL5580 www.deveerhoeve.nl

Accommodation: ☑ Pitch ☑ Mobile home/chalet ☐ Hotel/B&B ☐ Apartment

This is a family run site near the shores of the Veerse Meer, which is ideal for family holidays. It is situated in a popular area for watersports and is well suited for sailing, windsurfing and fishing enthusiasts, with boat launching 100 m. away. A sandy beach and recreation area ideal for children is only a five minute walk. As with most sites in this area there are many mature static and seasonal pitches. However, part of the friendly, relaxed site is reserved for touring units with 90 marked pitches on grassy ground, all with electrical connections. A member of the Holland Tulip Parcs Group.

You might like to know
The children will love the beautiful playground. In the school holidays, a dedicated activity team organises all kinds of events: crafts, games, dancing, musicals, talent shows etc.

- ☑ Multilingual children's club – pre-school
- ☑ Multilingual children's club – 5-10 year olds
- ☑ Multilingual children's club – 10-14 year olds
- ☐ Creative crafts
- ☑ Bicycle hire for children
- ☐ Facilities for children in wash blocks
- ☐ Children's pool
- ☑ Children's play area
- ☐ Crèche and/or babysitting
- ☑ Local information of interest for children

Facilities: Sanitary facilities in three blocks have been well modernised with full tiling. Hot showers are on payment. Laundry facilities. Motorcaravan services. Supermarket (all season). Restaurant and snack bar. TV room. Tennis. Playground and playing field. Games room. Bicycle hire. Fishing. Accommodation for groups. Max. 1 dog. WiFi. Off site: Slipway for launching boats 100 m. Riding 2 km. Golf 5 km.

Open: 1 April - 30 October.

Directions: From N256 Goes - Zierikzee road take Wolphaartsdijk exit. Follow through village and signs to site (be aware - one of the site signs is obscured by other road signs and could be missed). GPS: 51.54678, 3.81345

Charges guide

Per unit incl. up to 4 persons	€ 21,50 - € 24,50
incl. electricity (6A), water and drainage	€ 22,50 - € 25,50
incl. TV connection	€ 24,00 - € 27,50

NETHERLANDS – Kropswolde

Camping Meerwijck

Strandweg 2, NL-9606 PR Kropswolde (Groningen)
t: 0598 323 659   e: info@meerwijck.nl
alanrogers.com/NL5775   www.meerwijck.nl

Accommodation: ☑Pitch ☑Mobile home/chalet ☐Hotel/B&B ☐Apartment

This large lakeside site (23 ha), with 500 pitches (150 for touring units) is beautifully located on the beaches of the Zuidlaardermeer. The touring pitches are arranged on several separate fields away from the mobile homes and seasonal guests, either in circular bays or in long rows from paved access lanes. All touring pitches have electricity (6A), water, waste water and cable TV connections. This site is ideal for youngsters as there is direct access to the sandy beaches and there is an indoor heated swimming pool with a paddling pool. In high season an entertainment team provides games and excursions for youngsters and adults. Camping Meerwijck is a useful base from which to explore the surroundings of the province of Groningen and the bustling city itself is only 20 km. away and easily accessible by bicycle. The site has its own marina for 215 small sailing boats and motor boats and there is a slipway. Meerwijck is in a small nature reserve with good opportunities for walking and cycling.

You might like to know

In lovely natural surroundings, the site and marina are located at the beautiful Zuidlaardermeer Meerwijck. There is a lovely sandy beach and forest playgrounds. It is perfect for families with children, and for lovers of watersports, fishing, hiking and cycling. There are moorings for 215 boats.

- ☑ Multilingual children's club – pre-school
- ☑ Multilingual children's club – 5-10 year olds
- ☑ Multilingual children's club – 10-14 year olds
- ☑ Creative crafts
- ☑ Bicycle hire for children
- ☑ Facilities for children in wash blocks
- ☑ Children's pool
- ☑ Children's play area
- ☐ Crèche and/or babysitting
- ☑ Local information of interest for children

Facilities: Three modern and clean toilet blocks for tourers with hot showers (six minutes), washbasins (open style and in cabins), family bathrooms, baby rooms and facilities for disabled visitors. Laundry facilities. Small supermarket. Bar and snack bar. Indoor pool (15x20 m) with paddling pool. Playing field. Multisports court. Playgrounds. Animal farm. Tennis. Fishing. Bicycle hire. Marina. Activity team in high season. Lake with sandy beaches. Off site: Restaurant at the beach. Hoogezand 2 km. Zuidlaren 10 km.

Open: 1 April - 29 September.

Directions: On A7 to and from Groningen, take exit for Foxhol and continue south towards Kropswolde. Cross the canal and the railway and turn right at next roundabout towards the site. GPS: 53.14316, 6.68916

Charges guide

Per unit incl. 2 persons and electricity	€ 20,00 - € 27,00
extra person	€ 4,00
boat and trailer	€ 3,50
dog	€ 3,00

Camping De Pampel

Woeste Hoefweg 35, NL-7351 TN Hoenderloo (Gelderland)
t: 0553 781 760 e: info@pampel.nl
alanrogers.com/NL5840 www.pampel.nl

Accommodation: ☑ Pitch ☑ Mobile home/chalet ☐ Hotel/B&B ☐ Apartment

A site with no static holiday caravans is rare in the Netherlands and this adds to the congenial atmosphere at De Pampel. This is enhanced by its situation deep in the forest, with 9 ha. of its own woods to explore. There are 250 pitches (20 seasonal). You can choose to site yourself around the edge of a large open field with volleyball, etc. in the middle, or pick one of the individual places which are numbered, divided by trees and generally quite spacious. All have 6/16A electricity. The furthest pitches are some distance from the sanitary facilities. This peaceful park offers many opportunities for interesting outings with the two National Parks in the vicinity, the Kröller-Müller museum and the cities of Arnhem and Apeldoorn. Apeldoorn is particularly interesting as it is home to the Royal Palace of Het Loo, the Apenheul monkey park and the Juliana Tower. The area has good cycle paths which can be joined from a gate at the back of the site.

You might like to know

The indoor games area and part-covered swimming pool will keep everyone busy on site. There are lots of opporunities for days out at Apenheul primate park, Queen Juliana Tower amusement park, Burgers Zoo, the open-air museum and the national park.

- ☑ Multilingual children's club – pre-school
- ☑ Multilingual children's club – 5-10 year olds
- ☐ Multilingual children's club – 10-14 year olds
- ☑ Creative crafts
- ☑ Bicycle hire for children
- ☑ Facilities for children in wash blocks
- ☑ Children's pool
- ☑ Children's play area
- ☐ Crèche and/or babysitting
- ☑ Local information of interest for children

Facilities: Toilet facilities are good and modern, with free hot showers. Laundry. Shop (1/4-1/10). Restaurant. Snack bar (July/Aug, otherwise weekends only). Swimming pool and new fun paddling pool with water canon (heated by solar panels; open 1/4-31/10). Play area. Pets corner. Sports area. Indoor play area. Barbecues by permission only, no open fires. Dogs are not accepted in high season.

Open: All year.

Directions: From the A50 Arnhem - Apeldoorn road exit for Hoenderloo and follow signs. GPS: 52.111, 5.898

Charges guide

Per unit incl. 2 persons and electricity	€ 20,00 - € 30,50
extra person	€ 4,25 - € 5,25
child (1-11 yrs)	€ 3,25 - € 4,25

NETHERLANDS – Beerze-Ommen

Vrijetijdspark Beerze Bulten

Kampweg 1, NL-7736 PK Beerze-Ommen (Overijssel)
t: 0523 251 398   e: info@beerzebulten.nl
alanrogers.com/NL5985   www.beerzebulten.nl

Accommodation: ☑Pitch ☑Mobile home/chalet ☐ Hotel/B&B ☐ Apartment

Beerze Bulten is a large leisure park with all the amenities one could think of. Beside reception is a large, partly underground 'rabbit hole' providing a large indoor playground for children, a theatre for both indoor and outdoor shows and a buffet. Beerze Bulten has over 500 pitches, mainly for touring units, but also accommodation for hire. In the shade of mature woodland, all the pitches are level and all have electricity, water, drainage and TV connections. To the rear of the site is a large lake area with a sandy beach and adventure play equipment. Centrally located on the site is a full wellness spa centre. As well as heated indoor and outdoor pools, a fun paddling pool, jet stream, several different saunas and a water playground, this also offers full fitness facilities and a special salt cave treatment for those suffering from asthma or skin troubles. Beerze Bulten will provide a relaxing and active family holiday, and if the site doesn't offer enough, there is extensive surrounding woodland for walking and cycling.

Special offers
With the Giga early bird discount, the sooner you book the more you save! Visit www.beerzebulten.nl to see our prices.

You might like to know
Look forward to spectacular shows, great musicals and lots of fun in the Giant Rabbit Hole playground, home of Bultje the Bunny. The fun-filled entertainment includes original songs that will have adults and children alike singing along.

☑ Multilingual children's club – pre-school
☑ Multilingual children's club – 5-10 year olds
☑ Multilingual children's club – 10-14 year olds
☑ Creative crafts
☑ Bicycle hire for children
☑ Facilities for children in wash blocks
☑ Children's pool
☑ Children's play area
☐ Crèche and/or babysitting
☑ Local information of interest for children

Facilities: Several toilet blocks, well placed around the site, with toilets, washbasins in cabins and hot showers (key). Laundry. Shop. Bar and restaurant with open-air terrace. Snack bar. Heated indoor and outdoor pool complex and spa centre. Multisports court. Bicycle hire. Indoor playground and theatre. Playgrounds. WiFi. Full entertainment team in season and school holidays. Dogs only allowed on some fields.

Open: All year.

Directions: From A28, take exit 21 for Ommen and continue east towards Ommen. From Ommen, follow N34 northeast and turn south on N36 at crossing. Site is signed from there. GPS: 52.51139, 6.54618

Charges guide

Per unit incl. 2 persons and full service pitch	€ 41,50
extra person	€ 4,75
dog	€ 3,50

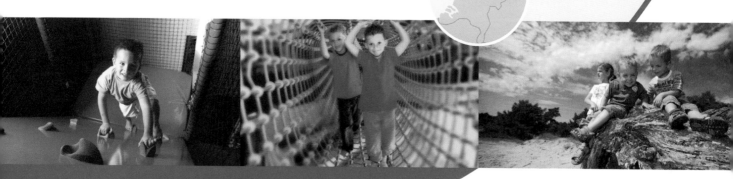

NETHERLANDS – Sellingen

Campingpark De Barkhoorn

Beetserweg 6, NL-9551 VE Sellingen (Groningen)
t: 0599 322510 e: info@barkhoorn.nl
alanrogers.com/NL6115 www.barkhoorn.nl

Accommodation: ☑ Pitch ☑ Mobile home/chalet ☐ Hotel/B&B ☐ Apartment

Camping De Barkhoorn is located in the Westerwolde southeast of Groningen. The campsite is surrounded by vast forests and heathland, interspersed with beautiful ponds. A car-free site, there are 152 touring pitches (including 13 'comfort' pitches) and pitches for motorcaravans, 82 permanent pitches and six cabins for rent. Tall trees provide plenty of shade. This is a pleasant family campsite, ideal for families with children. There are spacious green areas and in the holidays a recreation team provides entertainment and activities. There is a large natural recreational lake where you can swim. Adjacent to the site are a heated outdoor pool, an outdoor theatre and tennis courts. Many hiking and bicycle trails lead from the site and there are opportunities for fishing, mountain biking and canoeing. The Westerwolde area is rich in nature, culture and history. The German border is nearby.

Special offers
Special rates for a four-week stay for a family of four.

You might like to know
Camping de Barkhoorn is aimed at families with children under 12 years, who will love the entertaining characters chosen for our high season activity programme.

☐ Multilingual children's club – pre-school
☑ Multilingual children's club – 5-10 year olds
☐ Multilingual children's club – 10-14 year olds
☑ Creative crafts
☑ Bicycle hire for children
☐ Facilities for children in wash blocks
☑ Children's pool
☑ Children's play area
☐ Crèche and/or babysitting
☑ Local information of interest for children

Facilities: Four sanitary buildings including one without hot water. Private facilities to rent. Facilities for disabled visitors. Launderette. Shop. Bar and terrace. Restaurant. Snack bar. Swimming pool with slide and toddlers' pool. Play areas. Recreation lake with beach. Sports field. Minigolf. Tennis. Bowling and other activities. Bicycle hire. Fishing. Canoeing. WiFi. Cabins to rent.

Open: 1 April - 31 October.

Directions: Follow signs from Zwolle, Hoogeveen and Emmen for Ter Apel. Sellingen is on the main road between Ter Apel and Winschoten, 2 km. from the centre of Sellingen. Follow site signs from the village.
GPS: 52.946406, 7.131192

Charges guide

Per unit incl. 2 persons and electricity	€ 17,50 - € 22,50
dog	€ 3,00

Vakantiecentrum De Fruithof

Melkweg 2, NL-7871 PE Klijndijk (Drenthe)
t: 0591 512 427   e: info@fruithof.nl
alanrogers.com/NL6131   www.fruithof.nl

Accommodation: ☑Pitch ☑Mobile home/chalet   ☐ Hotel/B&B ☐ Apartment

Vakantiecentrum de Fruithof is an immaculately kept site that is attractively landscaped with different varieties of shrubs and trees. The site is fairly open and has attractive pitches on well kept grassy lawns with access from tarmac roads. They are separated by fir trees and low hedges, providing lots of privacy. De Fruithof has 450 level, numbered pitches (250 for tourers), all with 6A electricity, water, cable and drainage. To the front of the site is an open-air pool with a paddling pool and large water slide. In the centre of the site is a large lake with sandy beaches and some play equipment. In high season and school holidays, an entertainment team (with Flip and Fleur) provide activities for children. Next to the swimming pool is a comfortable restaurant with an open-air terrace. The area surrounding de Fruithof offers numerous opportunities for walking and cycling. Close by is the zoo in Emmen, the interesting village of Orvelte and the fortified town of Bourtange.

You might like to know
There is an extensive activity programme for all ages in high season, run by a professional team.

☐ Multilingual children's club – pre-school
☐ Multilingual children's club – 5-10 year olds
☐ Multilingual children's club – 10-14 year olds
☑ Creative crafts
☑ Bicycle hire for children
☑ Facilities for children in wash blocks
☑ Children's pool
☑ Children's play area
☐ Crèche and/or babysitting
☑ Local information of interest for children

Facilities: Four toilet blocks, well placed around the site, have toilets, washbasins (open style and in cabins) and free, preset hot showers. Washbasins for children. Family shower room. Baby room. Facilities for disabled campers. Laundry. Motorcaravan services. Shop (bread to order; open daily). Bar, restaurant and snack bar. Open-air swimming pool (heated) with water slide and paddling pool. Lake with sandy beach. Playing field. Tennis. Bicycle hire. Playground. Entertainment team (high season and school holidays). Off site: Emmen zoo.

Open: 8 April - 26 September.

Directions: On N34 take the exit for Emmen-Noord and turn immediately left towards Klijndijk. Follow site signs from there.
GPS: 52.828868, 6.857342

Charges guide

Per unit incl. 2 persons and electricity	€ 19,50 - € 29,50
extra person (over 2 yrs)	€ 4,65
dog (max. 1)	€ 2,75

Rivièra Parc

Spijkweg 15, NL-8256 RJ Biddinghuizen (Flevoland)
t: 0321 331 344   e: info@riviera.nl
alanrogers.com/NL6195   www.riviera.nl

Accommodation: ☑Pitch ☑Mobile home/chalet   ☐ Hotel/B&B ☐ Apartment

This Dutch Rivièra at the Veluwe Lake actually comprises two campsites with some shared amenities. Camping Rivièra Beach lies beyond the dykes, close to the water and the beach, while the bigger Rivièra Parc can be found within the dykes, with 1,195 pitches, 850 reserved for touring, all on grass and all with 4/10A electricity. There are also 450 serviced pitches (large with water, drainage and TV connection). The site boasts a very impressive range of facilities, even including a Snow Village with a snowtube. Other amenities are targeted at families with children up to 14 years, such as the covered play area and indoor swimming pool. In the wooded surroundings, opportunities for walking, cycling and riding are excellent.

You might like to know

Rivièra Parc is situated on the Veluwe, and its private sandy beach is gently sloping, making it ideal for children to paddle. They'll also have hours of fun in the indoor playground.

☑ Multilingual children's club – pre-school
☑ Multilingual children's club – 5-10 year olds
☑ Multilingual children's club – 10-14 year olds
☑ Creative crafts
☑ Bicycle hire for children
☑ Facilities for children in wash blocks
☑ Children's pool
☑ Children's play area
☐ Crèche and/or babysitting
☑ Local information of interest for children

Facilities: Good heated toilet blocks with separate facilities for babies and disabled visitors. Family rooms. Restaurants. Café. Snack bar. Takeaway food. Supermarket. Swimming pool with slide. Covered play area. Bowling. Bicycle and go-kart hire. Fishing. Amusement arcade. Internet access. Around 54 mobile homes and bungalows for hire. Off site: Riding. Watersports. Walibi World theme park 2 km. Golf 10 km.

Open: 1 April - 30 October.

Directions: Site is 2 km. southwest of Elburg. From A28 take exit to Elburg (N309). At Elburg follow signs for Dronten. Cross the bridge over the Veluwe Lake and immediately turn left (N306). Site is well signed from here and is on the left after 2 km. GPS: 52.44671, 5.79223

Charges guide

Per unit incl. up to 4 persons and 4A electricity	€ 28,00 - € 43,00
extra person	€ 5,75
dog	€ 4,75

NETHERLANDS – Zeewolde

Erkemederstrand Camping Horeca

Erkemederweg 79, NL-3896 LB Zeewolde (Flevoland)
t: 0365 228 421   e: info@erkemederstrand.nl
alanrogers.com/NL6200   www.erkemederstrand.nl

Accommodation: ☑Pitch ☑Mobile home/chalet ☐ Hotel/B&B ☐ Apartment

The Erkemederstrand (the beach of Erkemede) is a leisure park in Flevoland, with direct access to the Nuldernauw, a sandy beach, water and a forest. It provides a campsite for families, a marina, an area for youngsters to camp, a camping area for groups and a recreation area for day visitors. The campsite itself is divided into two areas: one before the dyke at the waterfront and one behind the dyke. The pitches are spacious (around 125 sq.m) and all have electricity, water and drainage. The focal point of the site and marina is the beach restaurant, De Jutter. This restaurant offers a varied menu for more formal dining, as well as catering for snacks, takeaway, ice creams or a cold beer on the terrace. There is plenty to do on the campsite, including a Red Indian village for the children where they can build huts, a children's farm and an extended programme of animation. Obviously with the proximity of the lake there are many opportunities for watersports.

Special offers
In the holidays, there is a comprehensive free activity programme with events for young and old alike (kids' club, disco, bingo, film, puppet-shows, wagon-driving, sports and games) and free use of the 3 km. long beach.

You might like to know
There are playgrounds, a bouncy castle, volleyball, children's BMX track, Indian village, canoe and pedalo hire, and much more!

☐ Multilingual children's club – pre-school
☐ Multilingual children's club – 5-10 year olds
☐ Multilingual children's club – 10-14 year olds
☑ Creative crafts
☑ Bicycle hire for children
☑ Facilities for children in wash blocks
☐ Children's pool
☑ Children's play area
☐ Crèche and/or babysitting
☑ Local information of interest for children

Facilities: Four neat and clean toilet blocks (access by key; exclusively for campers). Washbasins in cabins, showers and family bathrooms (free hot water). Dishwashing and laundry facilities in heated buildings. Shop for basic provisions. Bar, restaurant and takeaway. Several play areas and children's farm. Watersports facilities and lake swimming. Football pitch. Minigolf. Bicycle hire. Extended entertainment programme. Off site: Golf and riding 11 km.

Open: 1 April - 30 October.

Directions: From the A28 (Utrecht - Zwolle) take exit 9 (Nijkerk/Almere) and follow N301 to Zeewolde. Cross the bridge and turn right following signs to site. From Amsterdam/Almere, take exit 5 and follow N27 to Zeewolde; this road changes into the N305. Then take N301 to Nijkerk. From the bridge turn right and follow signs to site. GPS: 52.27021, 5.48871

Charges guide

Per unit incl. 2 persons and electricity	€ 22,50 - € 28,50
extra person	€ 2,50
dog	€ 2,00

NETHERLANDS – Heerde

Molecaten Park De Koerberg

Koerbergseweg 4/1, NL-8181 LL Heerde (Gelderland)
t: **0578 699 810** e: **info@koerberg.nl**
alanrogers.com/NL6355 www.molecaten.nl/dekoerberg

Accommodation: ☑Pitch ☑Mobile home/chalet ☐ Hotel/B&B ☐ Apartment

De Koerberg is a member of the Molecaten group and is located in the extensive Veluwe national park. This is a spacious site with large, well shaded pitches. Special hikers' pitches and simple cabins are available. Rentable accommodation includes safari style tents, and luxury mobile homes. The Dovecote restaurant has recently been added to the list of site amenities and offers a tempting range of local dishes (including takeaway meals). Breakfast can be delivered to your pitch if you wish. A bowling centre is also available and is great fun for a night out with a difference. A lively programme of activities and entertainment is arranged in high season. A children's club is held with many activities organised by the site's mascots, Molly and Caatje. Off site, there's plenty to do including a chocolate workshop and a bakery museum. The Kröller-Müller Van Gogh museum at Otterlo houses the world's second largest collection of the artist's work and is highly recommended.

You might like to know
The campsite has a forest location but the beach is easily accessible.

- ☐ Multilingual children's club – pre-school
- ☑ Multilingual children's club – 5-10 year olds
- ☐ Multilingual children's club – 10-14 year olds
- ☑ Creative crafts
- ☐ Bicycle hire for children
- ☑ Facilities for children in wash blocks
- ☑ Children's pool
- ☑ Children's play area
- ☐ Crèche and/or babysitting
- ☑ Local information of interest for children

Facilities: Shop. Bar, restaurant and takeaway food. Swimming pool. Play area. Tennis. Football. Bowling alley. Entertainment and activity programme. Mobile homes and chalets to rent. Off site: Riding. Cycle and walking tracks. Kröller-Müller museum.

Open: 1 April - 30 October.

Directions: Heading south from Zwolle, leave A50 motorway at exit 28 and follow signs to Heerde. Then follow signs to the site. GPS: 52.40965, 6.051149

Charges guide

Per unit incl. 2 persons and electricity	€ 19,00 - € 25,00
dog (max. 1)	€ 3,90

NETHERLANDS – Hattem

Molecaten Park De Leemkule

Leemkuilen 6, NL-8051 PW Hattem (Gelderland)
t: 0384 441 945   e: info@leemkule.nl
alanrogers.com/NL6358   www.molecaten.nl/deleemkule

Accommodation: ☑ Pitch ☑ Mobile home/chalet   ☐ Hotel/B&B   ☐ Apartment

De Leemkule is a member of the Molecaten group and can be found deep in the Veluwe woods. The camping area here is spacious and a number of 'comfort' pitches (electricity, water and drainage) are available. Hikers' cabins (for short term rentals) are set in beautiful, mature woodland. There is a real sense of nature here – sightings of rabbits and roe deer are common, particularly early in the morning. The mature Veluwe woods provide welcome shade in high summer, but there are also a number of sunnier pitches in fields at the centre of the site. With its 1,600 kilometres of dedicated cycle tracks, the Veluwe region has the most extensive cycle network in Europe (cycles for hire on site). Canoeing and walking in the 'De Weerribben and De Wieden' national park are also popular. The attractive old fishermen's village of Harderwijk is just 20 minutes away. In contrast, the Six Flags theme park and renowned dolphinarium are also close at hand.

You might like to know

Hattem is a great place for kids. There's a zoo and the 'bonbon atelier' is a workshop where you watch the art of chocolate making by a real chocolatier.

☐ Multilingual children's club – pre-school
☑ Multilingual children's club – 5-10 year olds
☐ Multilingual children's club – 10-14 year olds
☑ Creative crafts
☐ Bicycle hire for children
☑ Facilities for children in wash blocks
☑ Children's pool
☑ Children's play area
☐ Crèche and/or babysitting
☑ Local information of interest for children

Facilities: Restaurant and bar (with billiard table and a sunny terrace next to the outdoor pool), takeaway food. Supermarket. Indoor pool with children's pool and whirlpool, sauna, Turkish bath, solarium. Heated outdoor swimming pool with slides and water features. Tennis. Sports field. Play areas. Activity and entertainment programme including Molly & Caatje Children's Club. Bicycle hire. Dogs are not accepted. Off site: Walking and cycling. Harderwijk village. Six Flags theme park.

Open: 1 April - 1 November.

Directions: Take exit 17 from the A28 motorway, and follow directions as far as Wezep. At the roundabout in Wezep remain on N308 and continue ahead onto Stationsweg. The site is well signposted. GPS: 52.455587, 6.040238

Charges guide

Per unit incl. 2 persons and electricity	€ 18,00 - € 25,00
extra person	€ 3,90
child (2-10 yrs)	€ 2,90

Molecaten Park De Hooghe Bijsschel

Randmeerweg 8, NL-8071 SH Nunspeet (Gelderland)

t: **0341 252 406** e: **info@hooghebijsschel.nl**

alanrogers.com/NL6359 www.molecaten.nl/hooghebijsschel

Accommodation: ☑ Pitch ☐ Mobile home/chalet ☐ Hotel/B&B ☐ Apartment

A family focused campsite with direct access to Lake Veluwe, this site is understandably popular with windsurfers, sailors and fishermen. The lake is shallow and therefore also ideal for younger children. The camping fields are car-free and are bordered by hedges and mature trees. There is plenty of space for children to safely play in the middle of these fields. De Hooghe Bijsschel also has a range of fully equipped tents for rent. There is a marina and pier (with a slipway) – ideal for boat launching. In high season, special free courses in windsurfing and sailing are organised for children (to 12 years). Harderwijk is nearby – a delightful town with historic houses, an ancient street plan and a lively harbour. It's a popular destination for a shopping trip or people watching from one of the many pavement cafés. There are no fewer than three theme parks in the area – Six Flags, Julianatoren and Ecodrome. There are also more than 1,600 km. of cycle and walking tracks through the surrounding forests.

Special offers

During the summer holidays, there are watersports introduction mornings – free of charge for children aged 4 to 12 years.

You might like to know

Lake Veluwe is over 30 km² and is one of a series of man-made lakes known as the 'randmere', which were formed in 1957.

☐ Multilingual children's club – pre-school
☑ Multilingual children's club – 5-10 year olds
☑ Multilingual children's club – 10-14 year olds
☑ Creative crafts
☐ Bicycle hire for children
☑ Facilities for children in wash blocks
☐ Children's pool
☑ Children's play area
☐ Crèche and/or babysitting
☑ Local information of interest for children

Facilities: Restaurant and bar with terrace with lake view, takeaway food. Supermarket. Heated outdoor swimming pool with children's pool, whirlpool. Direct lake access. Beach with play area. Volleyball. Tennis. Play areas. Bicycle and boat hire. Windsurfing and sailing tuition. Activity and entertainment programme. Off site: Cycling and walking. Harderwijk. Six Flags theme park.

Open: 1 April - 1 October.

Directions: Take exit 14 from the A28 motorway and follow signs to Elspeet/Nunspeet on the N310. Upon reaching Nunspeet, continue ahead onto Elspeterweg/N310. On the outskirts of Nunspeet, take first exit on Vreeweg. Site is signed from here. GPS: 52.392054, 5.735056

Charges guide

Per unit incl. 2 persons and electricity	€ 17,50 - € 24,50
extra person	€ 3,90
child (2-10 yrs)	€ 2,90
dog	€ 3,90

Camping Gulperberg Panorama

Berghem 1, NL-6271 NP Gulpen (Limburg)
t: 0434 502 330   e: info@gulperberg.nl
alanrogers.com/NL6530   www.gulperberg.nl

Accommodation: ☑Pitch ☑Mobile home/chalet   ☐ Hotel/B&B   ☐ Apartment

Gulperberg Panorama is just three kilometres from the attractive village of Gulpen, midway between the interesting cities of Maastricht and Aachen. The 350 touring pitches are large and flat on terraces overlooking the village on one side and open countryside on the other. Many have full services. English is spoken in reception, although all written information is in Dutch (ask if you require a translation). Gulperberg Panorama is a haven for children; in high season there is a weekly entertainment programme to keep them occupied. The site is not suitable for visitors with disabilities. Dogs are restricted to one section of the campsite. Visitors are assured of a warm welcome and if arriving (or leaving) on a Saturday are welcomed (or bade farewell) by the 'Aartje Twinkle'. On site there are two outdoor swimming pools and a large, sandy play area where children are entertained. This is overlooked by a bar and restaurant and an attractive terrace with lovely views of the hills.

You might like to know
The campsite is in a forest location but the beach is easily accessible.

☐ Multilingual children's club – pre-school
☐ Multilingual children's club – 5-10 year olds
☐ Multilingual children's club – 10-14 year olds
☑ Creative crafts
☐ Bicycle hire for children
☑ Facilities for children in wash blocks
☑ Children's pool
☑ Children's play area
☐ Crèche and/or babysitting
☑ Local information of interest for children

Facilities: Four modern sanitary blocks have excellent facilities. Family shower room and baby room. Laundry. Shop (27/4-31/8). Bar. Takeaway. New restaurant with terrace. Swimming pool (29/4-15/9). Three play areas. Giant 'air cushion'. TV and games room. Extensive entertainment programme for children plus family entertainment. WiFi (charged). Off site: Golf and bicycle hire 3 km. Fishing 4 km. Riding 5 km. Further afield are caves, museums and Maastricht with its large variety of shops. Beach 15 km.

Open: Easter - 31 October.

Directions: Gulpen is east of Maastricht. Take N278 Maastricht - Aachen. Site is signed just as you enter Gulpen at the traffic lights. Turn right and follow camping signs for about 3 km. GPS: 50.80673, 5.89413

Charges guide

Per unit incl. 2 persons and electricity	€ 17,60 - € 23,60
extra person (over 2 yrs)	€ 2,40 - € 3,50
child (0-2 yrs)	free
dog	€ 2,25 - € 3,00

NETHERLANDS – Wanroij

Vakantiepark De Bergen

Campinglaan 1, NL-5446 PW Wanroij (Noord-Brabant)
t: 0485 335 450 e: info@debergen.nl
alanrogers.com/NL6635 www.debergen.nl

Accommodation: ☑Pitch ☑Mobile home/chalet ☐ Hotel/B&B ☐ Apartment

Brabant is an attractive holiday region, within easy access of large cities such as Den Bosch and Nijmegen. This is a well equipped site with direct access to a lake beach. There are four grades of pitch, ranging from the relatively simple 'standard' pitch to 'top of the range' comfort pitches (with 10A electricity, cable TV connections, water and drainage). Twin-axle caravans and units over 7.75 m. are not accepted. A range of chalets and mobile homes are available to rent. Several snack bars and restaurants can be found around the park, including Festina, a pleasant spot to watch the sun go down. A large leisure park surrounds the site and boasts a wide range of activities, including go-karts, minigolf, pedaloes and pony rides. A section of the lake has been cordoned off and is no deeper than 2 m. During peak season, bonfires are regularly organised on the lakeside. Bikes can be hired on site and there are many miles of excellent cycle trails through the surrounding countryside.

You might like to know
Children will love our exciting new themed playground based on the Jules Verne novel, 'Around the World in 80 Days'.

- ☑ Multilingual children's club – pre-school
- ☑ Multilingual children's club – 5-10 year olds
- ☑ Multilingual children's club – 10-14 year olds
- ☐ Creative crafts
- ☐ Bicycle hire for children
- ☑ Facilities for children in wash blocks
- ☐ Children's pool
- ☑ Children's play area
- ☐ Crèche and/or babysitting
- ☑ Local information of interest for children

Facilities: Snack bars and restaurants. Fishing. Pedaloes. Bicycle hire. Adventure playground. Bowling. Pony rides. Children's playground. Sports field. Activity and entertainment programme. Tourist information. Mobile homes and chalets for rent. Direct lake access (suitable for swimming). Off site: Overloon zoo and Liberty park 14 km. Grave (pretty market town) 14 km. Nijmegen (oldest city in the Netherlands) 36 km.

Open: 1 April - 31 October.

Directions: Head south from Nijmegen on the A73. Take the exit to Boxmeer and follow signs to St Anthonis. Here, head north on D602 to Wanroj, from where the site is clearly indicated. GPS: 51.64029, 5.81053

Charges guide

Per unit incl. 2 persons	€ 17,00 - € 28,00
electricity per kWh	€ 0,40
dog	€ 3,50

Molecaten Park Bosbad Hoeven

Oude Antwerpsepostbaan 81b, NL-4741 SG Hoeven (Noord-Brabant)
t: **0165 502 570** e: **info@bosbadhoeven.nl**
alanrogers.com/NL6655 **www.molecaten.nl/bosbadhoeven**

Accommodation: ☑Pitch ☑Mobile home/chalet ☐ Hotel/B&B ☐ Apartment

This is an ideal family site set in woodland with free access to one of Holland's most popular water parks, Splesj. Of the 900 pitches, 220 fully serviced pitches are for tourers; they are level, grassy, and mostly set in areas surrounded by mature trees with some hedge separation between pitches. There is a good restaurant with takeaway food, and with numerous play areas and a sports field there are plenty of activities for children if you can get them out of the water park complex. Only 5 km. northwest of the campsite, in the village of Oudenbosch, is a replica of St Peter's church in Rome! It took 25 years to build, is a little smaller than the original, but extremely impressive. Within the region there are plenty of other things to see and do and getting around in Holland is easy with its efficient autobahn network backed up by good main and country roads. In addition, being almost without hills it is a cyclists' paradise and full use should be made of the information and helpful advice available in reception.

You might like to know
The 'Indoor Skydive Roosendaal' is well worth a visit. And maybe try the parachute simulator.....

- ☑ Multilingual children's club – pre-school
- ☑ Multilingual children's club – 5-10 year olds
- ☑ Multilingual children's club – 10-14 year olds
- ☑ Creative crafts
- ☐ Bicycle hire for children
- ☑ Facilities for children in wash blocks
- ☑ Children's pool
- ☑ Children's play area
- ☐ Crèche and/or babysitting
- ☑ Local information of interest for children

Facilities: Three sanitary blocks, two modern, with all the usual facilites, showers charged by SEP key. Children's toilets and washbasins. Facilities for disabled visitors. Baby changing room. Washing machines, dryers, iron and ironing board. Motorcaravan service point. Supermarket. Restaurant, takeaway food. Covered swimming pool. Small lake with rowing boats and pedaloes. Train. Fishing pond. Tennis. Basketball. Sports field. Playground. Indoor adventure playground. Amusement arcade. Bicycle hire. Children's entertainment. WiFi (charged). Only raised gas barbecues permitted. Dogs are not accepted. Off site: Udenbosch with replica of St Peter's in Rome 5 km. Walking and cycle trails. Riding 6 km. Golf 12 km. Beaches 70 km.

Open: 1 April - 1 November.

Directions: Take exit 20 from A58 and follow signs to Industrieterrein Nijverhei St Willebrord. Turn right onto Heistraat and after 2 km. take third exit onto Bovenstraat. Turn right onto Oude Antwerpsepostbaan. The site is well signed from here. GPS: 51.570494, 4.560699

Charges guide

Per unit incl. 2 persons and 10A electricity	€ 17,00

NETHERLANDS – Lierop

Camping De Somerense Vennen

Philipsbosweg 7, NL-5715 RE Lierop (Noord-Brabant)
t: 0492 331 216 e: info@somerensevennen.nl
alanrogers.com/NL6690 www.somerensevennen.nl

Accommodation: ☑ Pitch ☑ Mobile home/chalet ☐ Hotel/B&B ☐ Apartment

De Sommersense Vennen is an attractive site which underwent a large scale renovation programme in 2006. A very good range of children's activities are organised here, based around The Twinkle Club, which are suitable for children of all ages. There are 125 touring pitches, and these are of a good size and generally well shaded. Most have electrical connections. A number of mobile homes and chalets are available for rent. There is a convivial bar/restaurant, serving the best pancakes locally! The impressive swimming pool complex (with sliding roof) includes a special children's area and a good range of children's games. There is a riding centre at the edge of the site with a large indoor arena. Off site, there is some excellent walking and cycling country across the Somerense heathland and further afield into North Brabant. Someren-Heide was formerly a mining town and dates back to the time of the Spanish Upper Gelderland. It is now a pleasant place to explore with a number of older buildings.

You might like to know

The beautiful swimming pool here is right next to the playground – guaranteeing hours of fun!

☐ Multilingual children's club – pre-school
☐ Multilingual children's club – 5-10 year olds
☐ Multilingual children's club – 10-14 year olds
☑ Creative crafts
☐ Bicycle hire for children
☑ Facilities for children in wash blocks
☑ Children's pool
☑ Children's play area
☐ Crèche and/or babysitting
☑ Local information of interest for children

Facilities: Swimming pool complex (can be covered). Bar, snack bar and restaurant. Riding centre. Children's playground. Children's club. Activity and entertainment programme. Tourist information. Mobile homes and chalets for rent. Off site: Walking in North Brabant. Shops, bars and restaurants at Someren-Heide.

Open: 26 March - 30 October.

Directions: Use A67 Eindhoven-Venlo motorway and leave at exit 35 (Someren). In Someren head towards Lierop and then follow signs to the site. GPS: 51.400403, 5.675804

Charges guide

Per unit incl. 2 persons and electricity	€ 19,50 - € 26,50
dog	€ 5,00

Molecaten Park Landgoed Ginkelduin

Scherpenzeelseweg 53, NL-3956 KD Leersum (Utrecht)
t: **0343 489 999** e: **info@landgoedginkelduin.nl**
alanrogers.com/NL6827 www.molecaten.nl/landgoedginkelduin

Accommodation: ☑ Pitch ☑ Mobile home/chalet ☐ Hotel/B&B ☐ Apartment

The Ginkelduin estate is located within the woods of the Utrechtse Heuvelrug national park. The park extends over 95 ha. and is an Area of Outstanding Natural Beauty consisting of woodland, moors and drifting sands. The car-free estate includes this high quality campsite, a member of the Molecaten group, with generously-sized pitches fringed with mature trees. A number of woodland pitches are equipped with individual sanitary units (containing a shower, washbasin and WC). There is plenty here for children, including indoor and outdoor swimming pools, a football pitch and a special bowling area. A number of fully equipped tents, chalets and mobile homes are for rent. The Utrechtse Heuvelrug has a royal heritage with magnificent gardens and castles. The nearby historic cities of Amersfoort and Utrecht, although maybe less well known, have a great deal of interest and are both important cultural and culinary centres. Miles of cycle paths criss-cross the area and bicycle hire is available on site.

You might like to know
This is a very tranquil site – a perfect spot to unwind and forget your day-to-day cares.

- ☑ Multilingual children's club – pre-school
- ☑ Multilingual children's club – 5-10 year olds
- ☑ Multilingual children's club – 10-14 year olds
- ☑ Creative crafts
- ☐ Bicycle hire for children
- ☑ Facilities for children in wash blocks
- ☑ Children's pool
- ☑ Children's play area
- ☐ Crèche and/or babysitting
- ☑ Local information of interest for children

Facilities: Restaurant, Bamboo garden with brasserie, snack bar and supermarket. Indoor swimming pool with whirlpool and Turkish bath, solarium. Heated outdoor swimming pool with slide, paddling pool and sunbathing area. Tennis. Sports field. Playgrounds. Minigolf. Bowling alleys. Bicycle hire. Information kiosk and Internet access point. Children's entertainment. Dogs are not accepted. Off site: Walking and cycle tracks. Utrecht. Amersfoort.

Open: 1 April - 1 November.

Directions: From the A12 motorway take exit 22 and follow signs to Woudenberg, Leersum and Maarsbergen. Continue on N225 as far as Leersum. After 1 km. turn left on Bentincklaan. Site is well signed from here.
GPS: 52.028336, 5.457705

Charges guide

Per unit incl. 2 persons, water and electricity	€ 21,00 - € 29,00
extra person	€ 3,90
child (2-10 yrs)	€ 2,90

Camping & Wellness Ons Buiten

Aagtekerkseweg 2a, NL-4356 RJ Oostkapelle (Zeeland)
t: **0118 581 813** e: **onsbuiten@ardoer.com**
alanrogers.com/NL6928 www.ardoer.com/onsbuiten

Accommodation: ☑ Pitch ☑ Mobile home/chalet ☐ Hotel/B&B ☐ Apartment

Camping Ons Buiten is a good quality site set amongst the landscapes of the Zeeuws, just 2.5 km. from the sea. The pitches are a minimum of 100 sq.m. and are serviced with electricity, cable TV, water and drainage. The pitch areas are kept free of cars with parking elsewhere. Ons Buiten is a destination for the whole family and plenty of activities are organised in high season for all ages. Little ones can play in the paddling pool and adults can spoil themselves at the site's excellent wellness centre. There are also plenty of activities nearby, the shops and restaurants of Vlissingen and the beautiful flora and fauna of Zeeland.

You might like to know

We are just 2 km. from the beach, dunes and forest, and the resort of Domburg. We offer a wide range of rental accommodation and generous pitches (some with private facilities). For children there is play equipment, an indoor play area and pool, and a professional activity team.

- ☑ Multilingual children's club – pre-school
- ☑ Multilingual children's club – 5-10 year olds
- ☐ Multilingual children's club – 10-14 year olds
- ☑ Creative crafts
- ☑ Bicycle hire for children
- ☑ Facilities for children in wash blocks
- ☑ Children's pool
- ☑ Children's play area
- ☐ Crèche and/or babysitting
- ☑ Local information of interest for children

Facilities: Toilet block including special facilities for children and disabled visitors. Launderette. Shared kitchen. Supermarket. Bakery. Café. Takeaway. Heated covered swimming pool. Play area. Sports pitch. Minigolf. Tennis. Wellness centre with sauna, salt cave and infrared cabin. Pets are not accepted. Off site: Beach 2.5 km. Golf 4 km.

Open: 14 March - 1 November.

Directions: From the A15 take exit 12 towards Middleburg and then the N57 for about 50 km. and join the N287 (Waterstraat) towards Oostkapelle. Site is well signed.
GPS: 51.56253, 3.54627

Charges guide

Per unit incl. 2 persons and electricity	€ 20,00 - € 59,00
extra person	€ 5,00

NETHERLANDS – Breskens

Molecaten Park Napoleon Hoeve

Zandertje 30, NL-4511 RH Breskens (Zeeland)
t: **0117 383 838** e: **info@napoleonhoeve.nl**
alanrogers.com/NL6935 www.molecaten.nl/napoleonhoeve

Accommodation: ☑Pitch ☑Mobile home/chalet ☐ Hotel/B&B ☐ Apartment

This site can be reached in less than two hours from Calais. It has direct access to a sandy beach, close to Breskens, best known for its fine Napoleonic fort. This is a high quality site with spacious 'comfort' pitches and the option of renting your own private sanitary unit. The main wash blocks are very well maintained, and children will enjoy taking a shower in a large ice cream cone! Leisure amenities include an indoor pool with water slides and a large indoor play area with all manner of play apparatus. Napoleon Hoeve is the flagship site of the Molecaten group and is a well maintained and well designed holiday centre. The surrounding countryside of the Westerschelde is very rural and best explored by cycle or on foot. However, a number of superb Belgian cities, notably Bruges and Ghent, can be reached within 30 minutes. The latter is sometimes overshadowed by Bruges, but is Belgium's third city and well worth a visit.

You might like to know
Why not visit the cheese farm in Oostburg or maybe the 'Visserij Museum' (fishing museum) in Breskens?

☑ Multilingual children's club – pre-school
☑ Multilingual children's club – 5-10 year olds
☑ Multilingual children's club – 10-14 year olds
☑ Creative crafts
☐ Bicycle hire for children
☑ Facilities for children in wash blocks
☑ Children's pool
☑ Children's play area
☐ Crèche and/or babysitting
☑ Local information of interest for children

Facilities: Two modern toilet blocks with toilets, washbasins (open and in cabins) and controllable hot showers. Special, attractive children's section with showers, basins and toilets. Private facilities for rent. Facilities for disabled visitors. Laundry. Restaurant with bar and terrace, takeaway food. Supermarket. Indoor pool with slide and children's pool. Play area. Games room. Indoor play area. Multisports fields. Bicycle hire. Activity and entertainment programme. Mobile homes and chalets for rent. Off site: Sandy sea beach (adjacent). Breskens 2 km. Knokke 7 km.

Open: All year.

Directions: Approaching from the south take the E40 motorway in Belgium (Brugge). At Oostkamp take E403, which becomes N31 and then N348 to Brugge and Knokke-Heist. Follow this road into The Netherlands, towards Cadzand and Breskens on N675. Pass through the village of Groede and take the first roundabout to the left towards the coast. Follow this road for 2.5 km. until you can only turn to the left. Site is signed here. GPS: 51.404113, 3.512768

Charges guide

Per unit incl. 2 persons and electricity	€ 15,00 - € 37,00
extra person	€ 3,90

Camping De Zeeuwse Kust

Helleweg 8, NL-4326 LJ Noordwelle (Zeeland)
t: **0111 468 282** e: **info@dezeeuwsekust.eu**
alanrogers.com/NL6948 **www.dezeeuwsekust.eu**

Accommodation: ☑Pitch ☑Mobile home/chalet ☐ Hotel/B&B ☐ Apartment

Camping De Zeeuwse Kust opened in April 2007. This new site is positioned on the island Schouwen-Duivenland, at the foot of the dunes and just five minutes from the well known seaside resort of Renesse. This site has 168 pitches which are spacious and comfortable. Some pitches have private sanitary provision. The sea offers plenty of opportunities for kite surfing, windsurfing and sailing and there are also plenty of walks possible through the dunes. There is a sailing school where you can have lessons. Whether you just want relaxation, something for the children, the seaside, or activities, you will find these all here. The recreation team organises several activities for children all year, such as treasure hunts, games, sports and arts and crafts afternoons. The outstanding, hotel standard facilities contained within the newly completed centrally located building are in a class of their own. An excellent heated pool and large indoor play area only add to the facilities offered at this site which is highly recommended.

You might like to know
Camping Strandpark De Zeeuwse Kust is a member of the Ardoer group, one of the Netherlands' leading camping organisations.

☑ Multilingual children's club – pre-school
☑ Multilingual children's club – 5-10 year olds
☑ Multilingual children's club – 10-14 year olds
☑ Creative crafts
☐ Bicycle hire for children
☑ Facilities for children in wash blocks
☑ Children's pool
☑ Children's play area
☐ Crèche and/or babysitting
☑ Local information of interest for children

Facilities: New, first-class sanitary building providing showers, washbasins, private cabins, family shower rooms and other facilities for children and disabled visitors. Launderette. Cooking facilities. Shop. Fresh bread (May-Sept). Excellent heated swimming pool. Play areas (indoors and outdoors). Entertainment team. Barbecue area. WiFi. Off site: Riding 500 m. Golf 7 km. Boat launching 7.5 km.

Open: All year (with most facilities).

Directions: From the A15 take exit 12 towards Middelburg. Follow the N57 through Ouddorp and then turn right on the N652. Immediately turn left for the N651 and follow to Nordwelle. Site is well signed. GPS: 51.73205, 3.79443

Charges guide

Per unit incl. 2 persons, electricity, water and drain	€ 17,00 - € 40,00
extra person (over 2 yrs)	€ 4,50

No credit cards.

NETHERLANDS – Rockanje

Molecaten Park Waterbos

Duinrand 11, NL-3235 CC Rockanje (Zuid-Holland)
t: 0181 401 900 e: info@waterboscamping.nl
alanrogers.com/NL6975 www.molecaten.nl/waterbos

Accommodation: ☑ Pitch ☑ Mobile home/chalet ☐ Hotel/B&B ☐ Apartment

Molecaten Park Waterbos is a small, friendly campsite located in sand dunes on the island of Voorne. The site is within easy walking distance of the broad sandy beach at Rockanje. This beach slopes gradually and is ideal for young children. Pitches here are shaded by large trees and are located on a number of grassy fields, often with play areas at the centre. There is a choice of basic, comfort and comfort 'plus' pitches. The latter group are deluxe pitches, each equipped with an individual shower, toilet and wash basin. Some mobile homes and chalets are available for rent. Waterbos translates as 'water forest' and this is a lush, dense forest with a myriad of narrow lanes and tracks to explore. It is a unique eco system with dozens of trees, shrubs, mushrooms, and birds which choose to nest here. The Voornes Duin is the dune's hinterland and there are some excellent cycle and walking tracks here.

You might like to know

Why not take a dip in the North Sea? It's calm in this area with some great sandy beaches.

☐ Multilingual children's club – pre-school
☑ Multilingual children's club – 5-10 year olds
☐ Multilingual children's club – 10-14 year olds
☑ Creative crafts
☐ Bicycle hire for children
☑ Facilities for children in wash blocks
☐ Children's pool
☑ Children's play area
☐ Crèche and/or babysitting
☑ Local information of interest for children

Facilities: Restaurant with bar and terrace, takeaway food. Small shop for bread and basics. Fishing pond. Play area. Bicycle and go-kart hire. Entertainment and activity programme. Dogs are not accepted. Off site: Beach adjacent. Rockanje 3 km. Sub-tropical swimming pool 10 km.

Open: 1 April - 1 October.

Directions: From Hook of Holland, follow signs to Rotterdam on the A20 motorway. At exit 13 follow signs to Rotterdam-Zuid (South), Hoogvliet. After 7 km. join A15 towards Hellevoetsluis, Europoort. Remain on A15, which becomes N15 as far as Rozenburg (12 km) and then take N57 to Hellevoetsluis. After 8 km. take third exit to the right towards Rockanje and follow this until this town. Go through the town centre and the site is signed. From the south, take A29 to Rotterdam, then take A15 to Europoort at the junction and follow directions above.
GPS: 51.879991, 4.053982

Charges guide

Per unit incl. 2 persons and electricity	€ 16,50 - € 22,00
extra person	€ 2,90
child (2-10 yrs)	€ 1,90

Camping Wulfener Hals

Wulfener Hals Weg, D-23769 Wulfen auf Fehmarn (Schleswig-Holstein)
t: **043 718 6280**   e: **camping@wulfenerhals.de**
alanrogers.com/DE3003   www.wulfenerhals.de

Accommodation: ☑ Pitch ☑ Mobile home/chalet ☐ Hotel/B&B ☐ Apartment

This a top class, all year round site suitable as a stopover or as a base for a longer stay. Attractively situated by the sea, it is a large, mature site (34 hectares) and is well maintained. It has over 800 individual pitches (half for touring) of up to 160 sq.m. in glades. Some are separated by bushes providing shade in the older parts, less so in the newer areas nearer the sea. There are many hardstandings and all pitches have electricity, water and drainage. A separate area has been developed for motorcaravans. It provides 60 extra large pitches, all with electricity, water and drainage, and some with TV aerial points, together with a new toilet block. There is much to do for young and old alike, with a new heated outdoor pool and paddling pool (unsupervised), although the sea is naturally popular as well. The site also has many sporting facilities including its own golf courses and schools for watersports. A member of Leading Campings Group.

You might like to know

For a small charge, our Children's Package will provide you with a travel cot, a child's bed and a high chair.

- ☑ Multilingual children's club – pre-school
- ☑ Multilingual children's club – 5-10 year olds
- ☑ Multilingual children's club – 10-14 year olds
- ☑ Creative crafts
- ☑ Bicycle hire for children
- ☑ Facilities for children in wash blocks
- ☑ Children's pool
- ☑ Children's play area
- ☐ Crèche and/or babysitting
- ☐ Local information of interest for children

Facilities: Five heated sanitary buildings have first class facilities including showers and both open washbasins and private cabins. Family bathrooms for rent. Facilities for children and disabled campers. Beauty and wellness facilities. Laundry. Motorcaravan services. Shop, bar, restaurants and takeaway (April-Oct). Swimming pool (May-Oct). Sauna. Solarium. Jacuzzi. Sailing, catamaran, windsurfing and diving schools. Boat slipway. Golf courses (18 holes, par 72 and 9 holes, par 27). Riding. Fishing. Archery. Well organised and varied entertainment programmes for children of all ages. Bicycle hire. Catamaran hire. Off site: Naturist beach 500 m. Village mini-market 2 km.

Open: All year.

Directions: From Hamburg take A1/E47 north direction Puttgarden, after crossing the bridge to Fehmarn first exit to the right to Avendorf In Avendorf turn left and follow the signs for Wulfen and the site. GPS: 54.40805, 11.17374

Charges guide

Per unit incl. 2 persons and electricity	€ 14,60 - € 42,11
extra person	€ 4,10 - € 8,60
child (2-13 yrs)	€ 2,30 - € 2,80
child (14-18 yrs)	€ 3,60 - € 7,40

Strandcamping Wallnau

Wallnau 1, D-23769 Fehmarn (Schleswig-Holstein)
t: **043 729 456** e: **wallnau@strandcamping.de**
alanrogers.com/DE3007 www.strandcamping.de

Accommodation: ☑ Pitch ☑ Mobile home/chalet ☐ Hotel/B&B ☐ Apartment

With direct beach access and protected from the wind by a dyke, this family site is on Germany's second largest island (since 1963 joined to the Baltic sea coast by a bridge). This is a quiet location on the western part of Fehmarn Island in close proximity to a large bird sanctuary. Of the 800 pitches, 400 are for touring, all with electricity and on level grass areas arranged in alleys and separated by hedges. The island is low lying, ideal for leisurely walking or bicycle riding, especially along the track that runs along the top of the dyke. The beach is a mixture of sand and pebbles and in summer lifeguards are on duty. The southern part is a naturist area. For those with an ornithological interest the bird sanctuary with over 80 species is worth visiting. Swimming, sailing and diving are possible in the sea and there is a windsurfing school. For those who prefer dry land there is pony riding for children and a riding school. During summer there are entertainment programmes for children and courses for adults.

You might like to know

Riding is popular here, with opportunities for all ages.

☐ Multilingual children's club – pre-school
☑ Multilingual children's club – 5-10 year olds
☑ Multilingual children's club – 10-14 year olds
☑ Creative crafts
☐ Bicycle hire for children
☑ Facilities for children in wash blocks
☐ Children's pool
☑ Children's play area
☐ Crèche and/or babysitting
☑ Local information of interest for children

Facilities: Heated sanitary blocks (cleaning variable) provide free showers. Child-sized toilets and showers. Baby rooms. Facilities for disabled visitors. Laundry facilities. Motorcaravan service points. Shop. Bar, restaurant and snack bar. Open-air stage and soundproofed disco. Health/cure centre, solarium and sauna. Archery. Watersports. Minigolf. Internet café. Beach fishing. Riding. WiFi (charged). Off site: Boat launching 6 km. Golf 15 km.

Open: 27 March - 25 October.

Directions: After crossing the bridge follow road to Landkirchen and Petersdorf. From Petersdorf site is signed. It is 4 km. northwest of the town. GPS: 54.48761, 11.0186

Charges guide

Per unit incl. 2 persons and electricity	€ 18,00 - € 35,30
child (under 17 yrs)	€ 2,00 - € 6,30
extra person	€ 4,00 - € 7,40

No credit cards.

Ferien-Campingplatz Münstertal

Dietzelbachstrasse 6, D-79244 Münstertal (Baden-Württemberg)
t: 076 367 080 e: info@camping-muenstertal.de
alanrogers.com/DE3450 www.camping-muenstertal.de/

Accommodation: ☑ Pitch ☑ Mobile home/chalet ☐ Hotel/B&B ☐ Apartment

Münstertal is an impressive site pleasantly situated in a valley on the western edge of the Black Forest. It has been one of the top graded sites in Germany for 20 years, and first time visitors will soon realise why when they see the standard of the facilities here. There are 305 individual pitches in two areas, either side of the entrance road on flat gravel, their size varying from 70-100 sq.m. All have electricity (16A) and 200 have drains, many also with water, TV and radio connections. The large indoor pool with sauna and solarium, and the outdoor pool, are both heated and free. There is a large, grass sunbathing area. The health and fitness centre provides a range of treatments, massages, etc. Children are very well catered for here with a play area and play equipment, tennis courts, minigolf, a games room with table tennis, table football and pool table and fishing. Riding is popular and the site has its own stables. The latest addition is an ice rink for skating and ice hockey in winter.

You might like to know

Bicycles can be hired on site (for both adults and children) – it's the best way to explore the Black Forest.

- ☐ Multilingual children's club – pre-school
- ☑ Multilingual children's club – 5-10 year olds
- ☑ Multilingual children's club – 10-14 year olds
- ☐ Creative crafts
- ☑ Bicycle hire for children
- ☑ Facilities for children in wash blocks
- ☑ Children's pool
- ☑ Children's play area
- ☐ Crèche and/or babysitting
- ☑ Local information of interest for children

Facilities: Three toilet blocks are of truly first class quality, with washbasins in cabins, showers, baby bath, a unit for disabled visitors and individual bathrooms, some for hire. Dishwashers in two blocks. Laundry. Drying room. Motorcaravan services. Well stocked shop (all year). Restaurant, particularly good (closed Nov). Heated swimming pools: indoor all year, outdoor with children's area. New health and fitness centre. Sauna and solarium. Games room. Bicycle hire. Tennis courses in summer. Riding. Ice rink (in winter). WiFi throughout (charged). Off site: Village amenities and train station next to site entrance. Golf 15 km. Freiburg and Basel easy driving distances for day trips.

Open: All year.

Directions: Münstertal is south of Freiburg. From A5 autobahn take exit 64, turn southeast via Bad Krozingen and Staufen and continue 5 km. to the start of Münstertal, where site is signed from the main road on the left. GPS: 47.85973, 7.76375

Charges guide

Per unit incl. 2 persons and services	€ 24,30 - € 29,50
extra person	€ 6,80 - € 7,90
child (2-10 yrs)	€ 4,50 - € 4,95

Maestro cards accepted.

GERMANY – Neuenburg-am-Rhein

Gugel's Dreiländer Camping

Oberer Wald 3, D-79395 Neuenburg-am-Rhein (Baden-Württemberg)
t: 076 317 719 e: info@camping-gugel.de
alanrogers.com/DE3455 www.camping-gugel.de

Accommodation: ☑ Pitch ☑ Mobile home/chalet ☑ Hotel/B&B ☐ Apartment

Set in natural heath and woodland, Gugel's is an attractive site with 220 touring pitches, either in small clearings in the trees, in open areas or on a hardstanding section used for overnight stays. All have electricity (16A), and some also have water, waste water and satellite TV connections. Opposite is a meadow where late arrivals and early departures may spend the night. There may be some road noise near the entrance. The site may become very busy in high season and on Bank Holidays but you should always find room. The excellent pool and wellness complex add to the attraction of this all year site. There is a social room with satellite TV where guests are welcomed with a glass of wine and a slide presentation of the attractions of the area. The Rhine is within walking distance. Neuenburg is ideally placed not only for enjoying and exploring the south of the Black Forest, but also when travelling from Frankfurt to Basel on the A5 autobahn.

You might like to know
Basel, Freiburg, Colmar and Breisach, four superb medieval cities, are all within easy reach.

☐ Multilingual children's club – pre-school
☑ Multilingual children's club – 5-10 year olds
☑ Multilingual children's club – 10-14 year olds
☑ Creative crafts
☐ Bicycle hire for children
☑ Facilities for children in wash blocks
☑ Children's pool
☑ Children's play area
☐ Crèche and/or babysitting
☐ Local information of interest for children

Facilities: Three good quality, heated sanitary blocks include some washbasins in cabins. Baby room. Facilities for disabled visitors. Laundry facilities. Motorcaravan services. Shop. Excellent restaurant. Takeaway (weekends and daily in high season). Wellness centre. Indoor/outdoor pool. Boules. Tennis. Fishing. Minigolf. Barbecue. Beach bar. Bicycle hire. Community room with TV. Activity programme (high season). Play areas. Off site: Riding 1.5 km. Golf 5 km. Neuenburg, Breisach, Freiburg, Basel and the Black Forest.

Open: All year.

Directions: From autobahn A5 take Neuenburg exit, turn left, then almost immediately left at traffic lights, left at next junction and follow signs for 2 km. to site (called 'Neuenburg' on most signs). GPS: 47.79693, 7.55

Charges guide

Per unit incl. 2 persons and electricity	€ 22,00 - € 26,50
extra person	€ 6,50
child (2-15 yrs)	€ 3,00
dog	€ 3,00

Hegau Familien Camping

An der Sonnenhalde 1, D-78250 Tengen (Baden-Württemberg)
t: 077 369 2470   e: info@hegau-camping.de
alanrogers.com/DE3490   www.hegau-camping.de

Accommodation: ☑ Pitch   ☑ Mobile home/chalet   ☐ Hotel/B&B   ☐ Apartment

Located in the sunny southwest corner of Germany, this site, new in 2003, must be one of the best we have seen. It is ultra modern in design and exceptionally high standards are maintained. Located in meadowland in a quiet rural valley close to the Swiss border, it provides excellent opportunities for walking, cycling and sightseeing. All 140 touring pitches (out of a total of 170) have electricity (16A), water and drainage, although water points are shared. The pitches are grassy and level and of a good size. At the bottom of the site is an excellent indoor heated swimming pool with a whirlpool and jacuzzi, a sauna and Turkish bath. A new large indoor playroom has recently been added. It is quite evident that the owners have succeeded in their aim to create a first class site for happy family holidays. With the Swiss border only minutes away, it is well placed for visits to Schaffhausen and even as far afield as Zurich. It is also an excellent spot to rest from touring the southern Black Forest which is a drive of less than an hour to the west.

You might like to know

Hegau was the first campsite in Baden-Württemberg to receive the 'Q' award for quality service.

- ☑ Multilingual children's club – pre-school
- ☑ Multilingual children's club – 5-10 year olds
- ☑ Multilingual children's club – 10-14 year olds
- ☑ Creative crafts
- ☐ Bicycle hire for children
- ☑ Facilities for children in wash blocks
- ☑ Children's pool
- ☑ Children's play area
- ☐ Crèche and/or babysitting
- ☑ Local information of interest for children

Facilities: New heated sanitary facilities include private cabins, showers, facilities for disabled visitors and for children. Three family shower rooms for rent (two also have a bath). Laundry facilities. Motorcaravan service point. Good value restaurant, small shop and bar opposite reception. Indoor swimming pool, sauna and Turkish bath (charged). Games rooms with TV and computer. Play areas and new indoor play room with bouncy castle, trampoline and go-kart style track. Minigolf. Communal barbecue pit. Free WiFi throughout. Off site: Golf 20 km. Skiing for children possible in the adjoining meadows. Supermarket less than 1 km.

Open: All year.

Directions: From A81 take exit 42 on to B314. At roundabout in Tengen follow international camping signs. Turn right at supermarket on edge of village. From Kommingen follow camp signs turning left towards site at supermarket on edge of village. GPS: 47.8244, 8.65323

Charges guide

Per unit incl. 2 persons	€ 21,00 - € 35,00
extra person	€ 8,50
child	€ 6,00
electricity (per kWh)	€ 0,50

Camping Hopfensee

Fischerbichl 17, D-87629 Füssen im Allgäu (Bavaria (S))
t: 083 629 17710 e: info@camping-hopfensee.com
alanrogers.com/DE3670 www.camping-hopfensee.com

Accommodation: ☑Pitch ☑Mobile home/chalet ☐ Hotel/B&B ☐ Apartment

This exceptional, family run site is situated beside a lake in the beautiful Bavarian Alps, not far from the fairytale castle of Neuschwanstein. Although one can appreciate the mountain scenery from the 376 level, fully serviced pitches, it is more comfortably viewed whilst swimming in the 31 degree swimming pool on the first floor of the wellness complex. The wellness complex, which offers a full spa programme, and the sanitary facilities are arranged around a large courtyard adorned with cascading flowers, and beautifully decorated glass doors lead to the men's, ladies' and children's facilities. The site has an excellent restaurant and bar with views over the lake. The site is a comfortable base for summer tours and sightseeing in the Bavarian Alps, however, during winter or in bad weather the site has a full range of facilities under cover that include a cinema and 1,000 sq.m. play room/barn on two levels. This site is a credit to the owners who have designed and developed it over many years.

You might like to know

There's an excellent indoor play area here, ideal for football, volleyball and basketball – with a giant slide!

☐ Multilingual children's club – pre-school
☐ Multilingual children's club – 5-10 year olds
☐ Multilingual children's club – 10-14 year olds
☐ Creative crafts
☐ Bicycle hire for children
☑ Facilities for children in wash blocks
☐ Children's pool
☑ Children's play area
☑ Crèche and/or babysitting
☑ Local information of interest for children

Facilities: The exceptionally good, heated sanitary facilities provide free hot water in washbasins (some in cabins) and large showers. Separate baby and children's washrooms. Private units for rent. Motorcaravan services. Takeaway. Shop. Supervised courses of water treatments, aromatherapy, massage, etc. Sauna, solarium and steam bath. Playground and kindergarten. Large games room. Bicycle hire. Tennis. Fishing. Ski-Safari in winter. Small golf academy and discounts for two local courses. No tents taken. Off site: Riding and boat launching 1 km.

Open: 11 December - 6 November.

Directions: Site is 4 km. north of Füssen. Turn off B16 to Hopfen and site is on the left through a car park. If approaching from the west on B310, turn towards Füssen at T-junction with the B16 and immediately right again for the road to Hopfen. GPS: 47.60572, 10.68052

Charges guide

Per unit incl. 2 persons and electricity	€ 30,05 - € 33,80
extra person	€ 8,70 - € 9,90
child (2-18 yrs)	€ 5,30 - € 9,35
dog	€ 4,15

Camping & Ferienpark Havelberge

An den Havelbergen 1, Userin, D-17237 Gross Quassow (Mecklenburg-West Pomerania)
t: **039 812 4790** e: **info@haveltourist.de**
alanrogers.com/DE3820 www.haveltourist.de

Accommodation: ☑Pitch ☑Mobile home/chalet ☐ Hotel/B&B ☐ Apartment

The Müritz National Park is a very large area of lakes and marshes, popular for birdwatching as well as watersports, and Havelberge is a large, well equipped site to use as a base for enjoying the area. It is quite steep in places with many terraces, most with shade, less in newer areas, and views over the lake. There are 400 pitches in total with 330 good sized, numbered touring pitches (most with 16A Europlug electrical connections) and 230 pitches on a newly developed area to the rear of the site with water and drainage. Pitches on the new field are level and separated by low hedges and bushes but have no shade. Over 170 seasonal pitches with a number of attractive chalets and an equal number of mobile homes in a separate area. In the high season this is a busy park with lots going on to entertain family members of all ages, whilst in the low seasons this is a peaceful base for exploring an unspoilt area of nature.
A member of Leading Campings group.

You might like to know

Tipi village features a kids' corner and summer sleepovers. Restaurant stage hosts shows and musicals. Try your hand at circus skills and much more! Cots and high chairs can be hired. Children's club runs daily during April-October with activities for all ages.

- ☑ Multilingual children's club – pre-school
- ☑ Multilingual children's club – 5-10 year olds
- ☑ Multilingual children's club – 10-14 year olds
- ☑ Creative crafts
- ☑ Bicycle hire for children
- ☑ Facilities for children in wash blocks
- ☑ Children's pool
- ☑ Children's play area
- ☐ Crèche and/or babysitting
- ☑ Local information of interest for children

Facilities: Four sanitary buildings (one new and of a very high standard) provide very good facilities, with private cabins, showers on payment and large section for children. Fully equipped kitchen and laundry. Motorcaravan service point. Small shop, modern restaurant, bar, takeaway and wellness (all 1/4-31/10). The lake provides fishing and swimming from a small beach, and boats can be launched (over 5 hp requires a German boat licence). Canoes, rowing boats, windsurfers and bikes can be hired. Play areas and entertainment in high season. Internet access. Off site: Riding 1.5 km.

Open: All year.

Directions: From A19 Rostock - Berlin road take exit 18 and follow B198 to Wesenberg and go left to Klein Quassow and follow site signs. GPS: 53.30517, 13.00133

Charges guide

Per unit incl. 2 persons and electricity	€ 15,90 - € 31,50
extra person	€ 4,30 - € 6,80
child (2-14 yrs)	€ 1,60 - € 4,60
dog	€ 1,00 - € 4,60

GERMANY – Dresden

Camping & Freizeitpark LuxOase

Arnsdorfer Strasse 1, Kleinröhrsdorf, D-01900 Dresden (Saxony)
t: **035 952 56666** e: **info@luxoase.de**
alanrogers.com/DE3833 www.luxoase.de

Accommodation: ☑Pitch ☑Mobile home/chalet ☐ Hotel/B&B ☐ Apartment

This is a well organised and quiet site located just north of Dresden with easy access from the autobahn. The site has very good facilities and is arranged on grassland beside a lake. There is access from the site to the lake through a gate. Although the site is fairly open, trees do provide shade in some areas. There are 138 large touring pitches (plus 50 seasonal in a separate area), marked by bushes or posts on generally flat or slightly sloping grass. All have 10/16A electricity and 100 have water and drainage. At the entrance is an area of hardstanding (with electricity) for late arrivals. The main entrance building houses the amenities and in front of the building is some very modern play equipment on bark. You may swim, fish or use inflatables in the lake. A wide entertainment programme is organised for children in high season. There are many interesting places to visit apart from Dresden and Meissen, with the fascinating National Park Sächsische Schweiz (Saxon Switzerland) offering some spectacular scenery.

You might like to know
Tickets for local excursions are available from the campsite reception.

- ☑ Multilingual children's club – pre-school
- ☑ Multilingual children's club – 5-10 year olds
- ☑ Multilingual children's club – 10-14 year olds
- ☑ Creative crafts
- ☑ Bicycle hire for children
- ☑ Facilities for children in wash blocks
- ☐ Children's pool
- ☑ Children's play area
- ☐ Crèche and/or babysitting
- ☑ Local information of interest for children

Facilities: A well equipped building provides modern, heated facilities with private cabins, a family room, baby room, units for disabled visitors and two bathrooms for hire. Jacuzzi. Kitchen. Gas supplies. Motorcaravan services. Shop and bar (1/3-31/12) plus restaurant (15/3-31/12). Bicycle hire. Lake swimming. Sports field. Fishing. Play area. Sauna. Train, bus and theatre tickets from reception. Internet point. WiFi. Minigolf. Fitness room. Regular guided bus trips to Dresden, Prague etc. Off site: Riding next door (lessons available). Public transport to Dresden 1 km. Golf 7.5 km. Nearby dinosaur park, zoo and indoor karting etc.

Open: 1 March - 31 December.

Directions: Site is 17 km. northeast of Dresden. From the A4 (Dresden - Görlitz) take exit 85 (Pulnitz) and travel south towards Radeberg. Pass through Leppersdorf and site is signed to the left. Follow signs for Kleinröhrsdorf and camping. Site is 4 km. from the autobahn exit. GPS: 51.120401, 13.980103

Charges guide

Per unit incl. 2 persons and electricity	€ 20,10 - € 29,50
extra person	€ 5,00 - € 7,80
child (3-15 yrs)	€ 2,50 - € 4,50

DENMARK – Blavand

Hvidbjerg Strand Camping

Hvidbjerg Strandvej 27, DK-6857 Blavand (Ribe)
t: 75 27 90 40 e: info@hvidbjerg.dk
alanrogers.com/DK2010 www.hvidbjerg.dk

Accommodation: ☑Pitch ☑Mobile home/chalet ☐ Hotel/B&B ☐ Apartment

A family owned TopCamp holiday site, Hvidbjerg Strand is on the west coast near Blåvands Huk, 43 km. from Esbjerg. It is a high quality, seaside site with a wide range of amenities. Most of the 570 pitches have electricity (6/10A) and the 130 'comfort' pitches also have water, drainage and satellite TV. To the rear of the site, 70 new, fully serviced pitches have been developed, some up to 250 sq. m. and 16 with private sanitary facilities. Most pitches are individual and divided by hedges, in rows on flat sandy grass, with areas also divided by small trees and hedges. On-site leisure facilities include an indoor suite of supervised playrooms designed for all ages, with Lego, computers, video games, TV, etc. and an impressive, tropical style indoor pool complex. This includes stalactite caves and a 70 m. water chute, the 'black hole' with sounds and lights, plus water slides, spa baths, Turkish bath and a sauna. A Blue Flag beach and windsurfing school are adjacent to the site. A member of Leading Campings Group.

You might like to know

Legoland is always great fun and makes an enjoyable day trip from site.

- ☑ Multilingual children's club – pre-school
- ☑ Multilingual children's club – 5-10 year olds
- ☑ Multilingual children's club – 10-14 year olds
- ☑ Creative crafts
- ☐ Bicycle hire for children
- ☑ Facilities for children in wash blocks
- ☑ Children's pool
- ☑ Children's play area
- ☐ Crèche and/or babysitting
- ☑ Local information of interest for children

Facilities: Five superb toilet units include washbasins (many in cubicles), roomy showers, spa baths, suites for disabled visitors, family bathrooms, kitchens and laundry facilities. The most recent units include a children's bathroom decorated with dinosaurs and Disney characters, and racing car baby baths. Motorcaravan services. Supermarket. Café/restaurant. TV rooms. Pool complex, solarium and sauna. Play areas. Supervised play rooms (09.00-16.00 daily). Barbecue areas. Minigolf. Riding (Western style). Fishing. Dog showers. ATM machine. Off site: Legoland 70 km.

Open: 19 March - 24 October.

Directions: From Varde take roads 181/431 to Blåvand. Site is signed left on entering the town (mind speed bump on town boundary). GPS: 55.54600, 8.13507

Charges guide

Per unit incl. 2 persons and electricity	DKK 220 - 365
extra person	DKK 75
child (0-11 yrs)	DKK 55
dog	DKK 27

Klim Strand Camping

Havvejen 167, Klim Strand, DK-9690 Fjerritslev (Nordjylland)
t: 98 22 53 40   e: ksc@klim-strand.dk
alanrogers.com/DK2170   www.klim-strand.dk

Accommodation: ☑ Pitch ☑ Mobile home/chalet ☐ Hotel/B&B ☐ Apartment

A large family holiday site right beside the sea, Klim Strand is a paradise for children. It is a privately owned TopCamp site with a full complement of quality facilities, including its own fire engine and trained staff. The site has 460 numbered touring pitches, all with electricity (10A), laid out in rows, many divided by trees and hedges and shade in parts. Some 220 of these are fully serviced with electricity, water, drainage and TV hook-up. On site activities include an outdoor water slide complex, an indoor pool, tennis courts and pony riding (all free). A wellness spa centre is a recent addition. For children there are numerous play areas, an adventure playground with aerial cable ride and a roller skating area. There is a kayak school and a large bouncy castle for toddlers. Live music and dancing are organised twice a week in high season. Suggested excursions include trips to offshore islands, visits to local potteries, a brewery museum and birdwatching on the Bygholm Vejle. A member of Leading Campings Group.

You might like to know
Fishing is popular here with all ages, either from the beach or on a boat trip out to sea.

- ☑ Multilingual children's club – pre-school
- ☑ Multilingual children's club – 5-10 year olds
- ☑ Multilingual children's club – 10-14 year olds
- ☑ Creative crafts
- ☐ Bicycle hire for children
- ☑ Facilities for children in wash blocks
- ☐ Children's pool
- ☑ Children's play area
- ☐ Crèche and/or babysitting
- ☑ Local information of interest for children

Facilities: Two good, large, heated toilet blocks are central, with spacious showers and some washbasins in cubicles. Separate children's room. Baby rooms. Bathrooms for families (some charged) and disabled visitors. Two smaller units are by reception and beach. Laundry. Well equipped kitchens and barbecue areas. TV lounges. Motorcaravan services. Pizzeria. Supermarket, restaurant and bar (all season). Pool complex. Sauna, solariums, whirlpool bath, hairdressing rooms, fitness room. Wellness centre. Internet cafe. TV rental. Play areas. Crèche. Bicycle hire. Cabins to rent. Off site: Golf 10 km. Boat launching 25 km.

Open: 26 March - 24 October.

Directions: Turn off Thisted - Fjerritslev 11 road to Klim from where site is signed.
GPS: 57.133333, 9.166667

Charges guide

Per unit incl. 2 persons and electricity	DKK 305 - 355
extra person	DKK 75
child (1-11 yrs)	DKK 55
dog	DKK 25

Been to any good campsites lately?
We have

You'll find them here...

... also here...

101 great campsites, ideal for your specific hobby,
pastime or passion

Want independent campsite reviews at your fingertips?

You'll find them here...

Over 3,000 in-depth campsite reviews at **www.alanrogers.com**

...and even here...

NOW ON ANDROID TOO

An exciting free app from iTunes, the Apple app store or the Android Market

Want to book your holiday on one of Europe's top campsites?

We can do it for you. No problem.

The best campsites in the most popular regions - we'll take care of everything

alan rogers

Discover the best campsites in Europe
with Alan Rogers

alanrogers.com
01580 214000

index

index

NETHERLANDS

index